HOW TO BE THE LORD'S PRAYER

Norman K. Elliott

HOW
TO BE
THE LORD'S
PRAYER

WORD BOOKS
PUBLISHER
WACO, TEXAS

HOW TO BE THE LORD'S PRAYER

Scripture quotations are from the Revised Standard Version of the Bible, copyright 1946, 1952, © 1971, 1973 by the Division of Christian Education of the National Council of the Churches of Christ in the U.S.A., and are used by permission.

ISBN 0-8499-2851-6
Library of Congress catalog card number: 78-20624
Printed in the United States of America

TO MY WIFE,
   MARION LOUISE

TO MY SONS,
   GLENN ROBERT and JAMES CLARK

TO MY DAUGHTER,
   KATHLEEN LOUISE

> *Whose love and patience
> have made life good*

Introduction

Norman K. Elliott has been a great Christian influence in my life, and I love his writings.

How to Be the Lord's Prayer had a revolutionary effect on my prayer life. Prayer is not the magic of certain words. In the deep down within us, prayer is what we are. And what we are is as much our aspirations and yearnings and unfulfillments as it is our achievements. We are the incarnation of our real prayer life.

Jesus is the Lord of the Lord's Prayer, and Norman says the words reveal the interior Jesus, and the God that was in Christ reconciling the world to Himself. As we look to Jesus and invite Him to sit on the throne of our lives, He expresses Himself in us and as us. He becomes all that we are, we are hid in Christ, and we are the very incarnation of true prayer. This is a thrilling and exciting discovery that changes our lives into centers of Holy Spirit activity. Now our every activity is prayer, our every word is prayer, and our every look is prayer.

How to Be the Lord's Prayer will accelerate your spiritual growth. It will expand your possibilities. It is an exercise in entering into the mind of Christ Jesus, and letting that mind be in you that was in Christ, expressed triumphantly as you. To understand The Lord's Prayer is to have a fuller understanding of all that Jesus is. *How to Be the Lord's Prayer* makes Jesus very real. To read this book, to put it into practice, makes Jesus a daily companion in the adventure of Kingdom living.

The book first of all describes the magnificence and the glory of God, His nature and His will—something so wonderful that we no longer fear God but reach out in eagerness to touch Him. Then it helps us to apply this magnificence to the practical affairs of daily living, just as The Lord's Prayer does, merging the spiritual with the practical, the heaven with the earth.

How to Be the Lord's Prayer added a new dimension to my prayer life. I wish every Christian, and every seeker after truth, would read it and take it to heart. Whoever does this will find life taking on a new wonder, and new closeness with the Lord of the Lord's Prayer, Jesus of Nazareth. His prayer life will become his entire life, and he himself "the hand of Jesus extended."

I recommend this book without reservation.

Ruth Carter Stapleton

Preface

THE FIRST DRAFT of this book was written during a speaking trip that took me from California to Boston, and then home to Minnesota. There was no intention when I began the trip to do any writing, but when some engagements fell through I felt that there was a reason for it, and while thinking about it one day the thought presented itself to my mind very clearly: "Why not begin now on the book you have been thinking about for so long?"

A few days later I actually began putting words on paper in the home of my brother-in-law, Miles Clark, in Altadena. Once I began, it seemed there was nothing to do but express what had been in my mind for so long. I continued my work in the home of Mr. and Mrs. David Brian, Sherman Oaks, California. A large part of the book was then written in Selma, Alabama, at the home of Mr. and Mrs. W. H. Sweeney. Another large chunk was written in the home of Mr. and Mrs. James Christian, Jr., in Lynchburg, Virginia. Part was written in the home of my brother, William Elliott, in Boston, Massachusetts. Another part was completed in New York City while visiting Mr. Robertson Smith, and but a few pages were left by the time I arrived home. To all of these close friends, I want to extend my gratitude for their patience and encouragement.

For typing, proofreading and many helpful suggestions I want to thank Mrs. George Mueller, Mrs. Gerald Roskilly, and Mrs. Helen McGovern. Their generous help has made the book possible at this time.

Norman K. Elliott

The Lord's Prayer

ONE OF THE first things that ought to be said about the Lord's Prayer is that it is not a prayer at all! Yet, when what is called the Lord's Prayer is rightly understood, it will make everything you are and everything you do *real prayer*.

There is no evidence in the gospels that Jesus ever used the words of the Lord's Prayer when He prayed. There are many references to the fact that He prayed often, and we even have some of his prayers recorded, but there is never a hint that He ever used these words in actual prayer, and this is rather unusual when we consider the number of times we speak the words over and over again. In fact, we say them so often that most of us are able to mouth the words without giving a solitary thought to their meaning, just as we can tie our shoelaces and be thinking about something else altogether.

When the disciples came to Jesus and asked Him to teach them how to pray, as John had taught his disciples how to pray, He told them to pray "After this manner [with these thoughts in mind] . . . ," and spoke the words which have become immortal and so greatly loved. The words, or rather the thoughts behind the words, contain His total attitude toward life—toward God, nature, man, life, the entire cosmos. He was saying something like this to them: "My friends, this is the way I see life. These are the ideas and the relationships I have found to make life worth living and meaningful."

E. Stanley Jones has said that the Kingdom of God is the kingdom of right relationships. The Lord's Prayer is the rationale that ushers us into this kingdom of right relationships. It is an exercise in entering into the mind of Jesus of Nazareth, in seeing life through His eyes, making decisions by His scale of values, and finding God in the light of His experience. The Lord's Prayer provides us with the means and the method whereby we can "Let this mind be in you, which was also in Christ Jesus" (Philippians 2:5).

Prayer, viewed in this manner, is life, attitude, meaning—the totality of one's personality meaningfully and rightly related to the totality of life. It is from this perspective that we shall attempt to understand the Lord's Prayer, to have the mind that was in Christ Jesus, to achieve a life that satisfies our deepest desires and releases our highest possibilities.

It must never be forgotten that the Lord's Prayer is the verbal expression of a man, "the Word made flesh." Our fullest understanding of the meaning of the words of the prayer is not enough, because the ideas and the attitudes are not ours, much as we might wish that they were. It is one thing to understand; it is another thing to *be*. The gulf between understanding and being can be so vast as to be utterly defeating and completely discouraging. Browning has said, "A man's reach should exceed his grasp." In our present state of development, perhaps this is the way it must be; but there is the vision and the truth of Scripture that merges vision with fact, idea with flesh: ". . . we shall be like him . . ." (I John 3:2). In that time we shall not merely understand the thoughts and words of the Lord's Prayer; *we shall be the Lord's Prayer.*

When we learn from someone else, our understanding often exceeds our ability to incarnate our understanding. An artist might give us freely and fully of all his knowledge, but we find out quickly that we also need the artist. Much of our knowledge confuses us. The ideas have not become flesh yet. And so we say, "I can't seem to do this. How do *you* do it?" So it goes, little by little, that through the generosity and skill of the artist, we become the artist.

In something of this fashion, we will learn to become the Lord's Prayer, but in order to do so we must walk with the Lord of the Lord's Prayer, Jesus of Nazareth—Christ Jesus our Lord. We have to accept His invitation, "Come unto me, all ye that labour and are heavy laden, and I will give you rest. Take my yoke upon you, and learn of me; . . . and ye shall find rest unto your souls." (Matthew 11:28). By association we shall be like Him, in the manner referred to in II Corinthians 3:18: "But we all, with open face beholding . . . the glory of the Lord, are changed into the same image. . . ."

In the process of learning and association we will often find ourselves in the same situation as the disciples who were unable to heal the epileptic and had to call upon their Lord, and were told that "this kind" does not come forth except by prayer and fasting. In their case, perhaps "the Word made flesh" in them had not caught up to their understanding and vision. They needed the Lord of the Lord's Prayer, and so it shall be often with us even after it seems that we understand it.

And so, as we try to plumb the depths of these ideas behind the words of the Lord's Prayer, let us do it with the continual prayer, "Help me, Lord Jesus."

Contents

HOW TO BE THE LORD'S PRAYER

1

Our Father Which Art in Heaven

ESUS' basic attitude is one of *personal identification with* God. One cannot look out on the universe without seeing and sensing something of the majesty of the Creator. Our minds reel at the immensity of space and the staggering stellar system. Although we talk in terms of billions of light years, in reality the mind is incapable of really understanding or appreciating what we are talking about. Even with the latest radio telescopes there is no limit "to the heavens." We can only vaguely sense what it means when astronomers talk not only about billions of stars, but about countless galaxies the size of our own Milky Way or much larger. In comparison to the totality of what is known, our own Milky Way is so tiny, and in comparison to the Milky Way our own sun is so small that it is practically invisible. Within our own solar system, the earth-planet we live on is very minor in size compared to the giants such as the planet Pluto. Yet we earthlings become so earthbound in mind that we usually tend to think of God in terms of this microscopic piece of cosmic dust we call the earth. God is so much vaster, greater and more magnificent. How great God is!

A scientist once told me that when the problems of life pressed too closely in upon him he had one way of putting things back into their place. "I put my eye to a telescope," he said. "Suddenly the problems of earth and the pressures of my own little personal world seem quite insignificant."

Man had done this long before the advent of the telescope. The Psalmist says, "When I consider thy heavens, . . . the moon and the stars . . ." (8:3). In this sentence one can almost see the young shepherd David, lying on his back on a hilltop at night, gazing in wonder and awe into the mystery of the night sky. In another psalm he says, "The heavens declare the glory of God . . ." (19:1).

The consideration of "the heavens" is good for a man or a woman. It is thrilling. It stretches our mind. It stimulates the imagination. But it can also be overpowering, dwarfing into almost meaninglessness the human personality. We need more than this.

Man has also learned something of the nature of God from the things of earth. The sequence of the seasons, the balance of nature, the facts of geology, the study of plant and animal life, the relationships expressed in mathematics, and revelations of chemistry and physics. Surely no one can make a study of any of these and really believe there is not a directive intelligence of awesome proportions and ingenuity behind and through life. And so the Psalmist says, ". . . and the firmament sheweth his handywork" (19:1).

A friend once told me that his first real contact with God came on a farm in Indiana. He had worked all day in the cornfields in the summer sun. After supper he sat on the porch in the relative coolness of the closing day. Stillness covered the twilight earth. Suddenly an ear of corn cracked and split the stillness with the voice of growth! His heart raced and his mind caught fire with the realization of the livingness all about him. Until that moment the cornstalks were inanimate and separated from his world of "life." Now they were one. An ocean of living life was all about him, and he was in the middle of it. But this was not all. The living cornstalks awakened in his mind the life behind the corn, the life that gave "life" to the corn-God!

The great scientist is ever aware of the something beyond his specialty. It is said that once a student entered the laboratory of Louis Pasteur and saw the great man bent over a table with his head bowed. He assumed that Pasteur was in prayer and waited in silence until he raised his head. As the scientist turned around he noted that he had been peering into a microscope.

"Oh, I thought you were praying."

Pasteur answered, "I was."

But even this awareness of God, good and necessary as it is to a thinking man, is not enough, because to most of us "nature" is something apart from ourselves. We are like spectators at a game. Wonderful as it might be, it is something that is "not us."

If we can understand all there is to know about the universe, and it still has no *personal* relationship with us, and if we do not have a human sense of integration with it, we are but strangers in the universe, alone and orphaned, regardless of how majestic it might be and regardless of how magnificent must be the God in and through and back of it.

Jesus assumed and claimed *personal identification* with that which is in and through and in back of the universe in the words, "Our Father." He did not explain it. He took it for granted. In a way He "voted Himself into" the family of life—wherever He looked. He used that which He had learned from life and from nature in a personal rationale that *included Himself* and was *applicable to Himself.*

In the Sermon on the Mount He talks about the lilies of the field and the grass. They were not obsessed with anxiety and yet their life needs were met. God had built into the pattern and fabric of nature the fulfillment of their lives, and we must have trust and faith that God has also provided for our fulfillment. Jesus is saying that it is quite unthinkable that somehow or other God "forgot" or was "unable" to provide for us in His plan of creation. He is also implying that we have much to learn from the flowers and the grass in accepting what is already provided for us in God's plan.

Wherever Jesus looked on nature He saw God or the operation of God, and He applied to man the lessons learned there. The references to nature in the gospels are quite numerous. He speaks of the birds of the air, the foxes, the fish, the rising and setting of the sun, the trees and the vines, the tares and the wheat, the sowing of seed, grapes; and in all of these He found the working of God applicable to man.

Jesus also saw God's nature in man's relationship with man. He talked about the man who built his house on the sand and the man who built his house on the rock. He had undoubtedly seen men and contractors do this very thing, but to Jesus it was more than a mere observation of the erecting of a building. In the relationships involved in such a project He also saw the working of God's laws. He talked about the woman who lost a coin, the widow and her mite, the farmer who had two sons, and many other stories involving people. In all of them He saw more than a commentary on human nature. He saw the revelation of God and His laws. This does not mean that Jesus viewed God as creation, or God limited in creation, but rather that God, though transcendent, is known to man in His creative immanence.

When Moses asked to see God he was told that no man could see Him, but that God would hide him in the cleft of a rock, and permit Moses to see His hind parts. So the glory of God passed by and Moses saw the hind part of God. What does this mean? One explanation is that no man can see Spirit, which is God, for God as Spirit is invisible. Perhaps the immanence of God was revealed to Moses in a most miraculous revelation of God in nature, in a more pure and unobscured sense than is permitted most people.

Margaret Prescott Montague had an experience of this sort. In the hospital where she was convalescing, she was wheeled out on the porch one afternoon. As she looked at a bird, suddenly it was as if the veil was stripped from creation and God was revealed to her in a most clear and intimate way. She called it "twenty minutes of reality." It seemed that she was seeing creation through the eyes of God, and it was arrayed in unspeakable beauty.

Surely these experiences, commonly called mystical, were not unknown to Jesus of Nazareth. When one is in personal union with God, he is actually in personal union with all God's creation.

So, at the beginning and always as the basis to Jesus' way of life is this personal identification in the words, "Our Father."

Through habit we associate prayer with the bowing of the head, the closing of the eyes, and the folding of the hands. When such postures are repeated numberless times, and when these numberless times have been associated with God and all that is sacred, we tend to equate the sacred with the posture. Thus when we open our eyes we tend to see and think of the "world" as different from "God." We split existence into sacred rites and secular activities. There was no such separation in the life of Jesus. He prayed at times with His eyes open, as when He "lifted up his eyes to heaven, and said . . ." (John 17:1). Even in the instance of the prayer prior to the raising of Lazarus, one gets the impression that it was unusual for Him to pray aloud, or at least so that others could hear Him. "And Jesus lifted up his eyes, and said, Father, I thank thee that thou hast heard me. And I knew that thou hearest me always: but because of the people which stand by I said it, that they may believe that thou hast sent me" (John 11:41-42).

In Jesus' mind God had already "heard" Him. This would be quite natural and normal for Jesus whose very life was prayer. Words and the closing of the eyes were mostly unnecessary.

An exercise which will tend toward personal union with God and His expression in life is to pray with the eyes open. If one will do it for thirty days he will find his world more friendly, and God a continuing and personal awareness. I have never seen it to fail.

As you sit in the kitchen, your eyes may be seeing a pile of dishes on the sink as you say, *"Heavenly Father. . . ."* Perhaps you will be looking at your child or wife or husband as your prayer continues: *"I thank You for this day and the health that enables me to go to work. . . ."* Now the refrigerator comes into your vision as you say, *"Bless my wife and children as they go about the duties of the day. . . ."* Your eyes might now be looking at the pattern of the linoleum as you say, *"Father, there is a sales meeting I must attend this morning. I thank You for the right ideas and confident assurance. . . ."* By now your eyes have shifted to the window and the trees outside as you say, *"Bless my efforts today. . . ."* The kitchen table with plates and knives and forks comes into view as you say, *". . . and make me a blessing to everyone I meet this day."* Now the stove stands in full view as you say, *"Amen."*

Of course this can be done any place, and the thought and attitude of prayer will soon encompass everything that comes into sight, be it a bus, building, sidewalk, laundry machine, or the clouds in the sky.

Something remarkable will happen to you during the thirty days of this experiment. *All life will become holy and sacred.* The sights and sounds that used to be distractions will suddenly become stimuli to the awareness of God. No matter where you are, or what you are doing, the whole world will be consciously God-filled. Life will become One for you.

Dr. George Washington Carver talked most lovingly of his "Mr. Creator." He always wore a flower in his lapel because it reminded him of God. He approached his experiments in chemistry with a humbleness amounting to an act of worship.

When he was an old man I met him in St. Paul, Minnesota, at the home of Dr. Glenn Clark. When he spoke of the peanut and all that he had discovered and made from the peanut, it was with childlike wonder. His respect and reverence for the life of God in nature was very much like the identification we are talking about. Certainly God was no distant Being to him, for George Washington Carver had found God in field trips and among the test tubes of his laboratory. He had a habit of tenderly touching the flower in his buttonhole and one could not help but think that this was an act of communion with his God. He had a delightful habit of quoting the lines of Tennyson:

> Flower in the crannied wall,
> I pluck you out of the crannies,
> I hold you here, root and all, in my hand,
> Little flower—but if I could understand
> What you are, root and all, and all in all,
> I should know what God and man is.

In this humble man one could almost hear the echo of Jesus from two thousand years ago: "Consider the lilies of the field . . ." (Matthew 6:28).

This identification is not limited by any means to the trees and the countryside. It includes the activities in which we are involved.

A successful insurance salesman prays each day before he leaves the house that he will reveal and find something of the goodness of God in every contact he has that day. He thanks God for the opportunity to make such calls, and he also finds God in them.

After every call he thanks his heavenly Father for the privilege of having talked with the person he has just seen. He does it whether or not a sale is made. The success or failure of the call, from a sales point of view, has nothing to do with his realization and appreciation that God is inextricably bound up in every facet of his life. It is not possible for him to separate life into religious and nonreligious compartments. God is in all, and He is all in all, for this salesman. He is God's man whatever he is doing, and God is with him and in all that he does. His very breath is saying, "Our Father. . . ."

The Apostle Paul said, "In every thing give thanks: for this is the will of God in Christ Jesus concerning you" (I Thessalonians 5:18). Most people feel that God is with them only when their efforts are successful. If we limit union and identification with God only to successes, then God will not be with us half the time. Not all of our efforts are successful, if by success we mean that we got our way and achieved our hopes and goals. That was not even true with Jesus. From the human point of view most of His efforts did not achieve what He desired. The leaders of the church turned against Him. The rich young ruler did not become His disciple, as far as we know. He knew tremendous popularity and He also knew the rejection and falling away of the crowds.

The goal of life is personal union with God, and hence with all life. True success is the constant awareness and experience of the Reality. It is very necessary, then, to get a better and more balanced view of "success." One man sows and another reaps, but both have entered into the same labor. The reaper would never reap if the sower had never sowed. It is true in business, scientific investigation, the arts, everything—everyone builds upon the efforts of others. It is especially true of the one who went before him. The thing to remember is that God was involved in the affairs of the first man just as much as He was with the man who finally receives credit for having "discovered and achieved."

In the life of prayer we have exactly the same story. There is no question but that many prayers by many different people at many different times is the history of everyone's life. They might be prayers for a new direction in life, for help in distress or for someone to find a job. It is a fallacy to think that the "successful prayer" was the one in which the person finally got help. It is thrilling and humbling to pray for someone and see the result of that prayer; but let us never forget that our "successful" prayer would never have achieved the results without many an unknown prayer having done its job. The success of the last prayer actually fulfills the prayers of all that went before it. God was as much involved in the "unsuccessful" prayers as He was in the prayer that tipped the balance. In the life of prayer we need the sower, the waterer, and the one who weeds as well as the reaper. Then we need something else, the climate to overshadow and mother the whole process. Just as the sower and the waterer and the weeder and the reaper would be fruitless without the sun and rain and chemistry of the soil, so, too, our efforts and prayers would be unfruitful without the overshadowing climate of the will of God.

Starr Daily, condemned to life in prison, had a vision of Christ and became a new man. He was released from prison even though he was not ever supposed to get out, and the warden had vowed it would never happen (likely with good reason). How can we account for it? Starr Daily has told me that he gives most credit for his release to his father. No matter what he did, no matter how many times he landed in jail, his father continued to love him and send up a stream of prayer on his behalf. The time came when the father died. Most people might believe that prayer ends then, but not Starr Daily. He says that he knows the love of his father continued and that his prayers were even more effective in heaven. Certainly Jesus was the same personality after the resurrection that He was before it. Why should it change merely because of the transition of death? Starr Daily is absolutely convinced that it was the prayers of his father continuing on the other side that brought the vision of the living and loving Christ into the dungeon and saved his life.

Which prayer of Starr Daily's father was the successful one? Would the last one have been successful without the lifetime of praying that went before it? Of course not. God was in and through them all; and eventually, in God's own good time, they all proved successful.

When we understand this, and by conscious attitude and dedication constantly live the reality of "Our Father," *we live and move and have our existence "in"* God.

What is heaven but the *reign* and *rule* and *manifestation* of the *nature of God?* As God has *always been, always is,* and *always shall be,* so *heaven always has been, always is,* and *always shall be.*

It is a great mistake to think of heaven as something that happens after we die. It separates us from the "here and now" which is "my Father's world," and separates us from our fellow man.

It is said that the Kingdom of Heaven is "within you" (Luke

17:21), that it is "in the midst of thee" (Zephaniah 3:17), that it is "at hand" (Matthew 4:17). We must claim it now, recognize it by faith, and live up to the standards of it to the best of our ability in order to be true citizens of this Kingdom of Heaven, and the children of God.

We get direction and instruction in the words of Jesus: "The time is fulfilled, and the kingdom of God is at hand: repent ye and believe the gospel" (Mark 1:15).

There are undoubtedly many historical considerations in this statement, but there is one individual concern that overshadows the historical. There comes the time in the life of every man of God when he claims this Kingdom as a *present-tense reality* in his own life. The Kingdom of Heaven is a continuing reality just as God Himself is a continuing Reality. The realization and understanding of this *"is-ness"* of God, His reality and His manifesting nature, is a necessary step! As long as our minds are set toward some distant time in which our dreams will come true, we will not enter into the glory of God that is always pushing in upon us, wanting to express and change. The Kingdom of Heaven is *here* just as much as it will be *there* in some indefinable and obscure future. In fact, *it is quite possible that if we do not discover the Kingdom of God in the "here," we will be unprepared to experience it in the "there."*

Just as the reality of God, that in which (and He in whom) we live and have our being, is in the "now-ness" of the entire creation, and just as the Creator is inseparable from His creation, so His "Kingdom" or "realm" is in the "here" and the "now."

This Kingdom is so close that to say it is at hand is truly an understatement. Jesus said that we were *in the midst of it;* and then to complete the picture of our envelopment in it He said it was *within us!* We are in it, part of it, and although we fail to see it, it is here nevertheless.

For one who is conscious of this reality it is difficult to understand those who are so close to apprehending it and yet always missing it. How Jesus groaned within Himself as He said, "You have eyes and you do not see; you have ears and you do not hear; you have hearts and yet you do not enter into understanding!" Frustration? Yes. Sadness? Yes. Yearning? Yes.

The first step toward entering this expanded consciousness is to decide that it is real and claim it. Become so dissatisfied that the life of your very soul can no longer wait for something in a veiled future. Throw yourself upon the ocean of life and demand reality now. The time to do it is always "now." There is no time in history that is any more sacred than another. There was no more of God in life during the time Jesus walked the roads and roamed the countryside of Palestine than there is today, at this very moment. There was no more of God breaking through into human lives during the time of Saint Francis of Assisi than there is at this very moment. God was no more powerful nor capable of entering into human affairs during the times of Luther, Calvin, Fox, Wesley or Mueller than He is at this very moment. It would have been no easier to find God at any of those "times" than it is right now.

We delude ourselves when we envy not having lived in another time of history. During the life span of any saint of God most of the population did not know God any more than they do today. The God-conscious and the God-dedicated are always a minority. Had we to wait for some sort of democratic process to vote in the Kingdom of God, we would simply wait! But in *every* age, at *every* time, there are *always* those who demand heaven now. Not that they deny the heaven of the hereafter, but they claim and know the reality of it as a continuing, constant, and eternal reality.

When a man is able to say, "The time is fulfilled *for me, right now*," he enters into a new relationship with the universe and the Creator of the universe. The present and the future, the spiritual and the material, merge into oneness. He may have to begin by assuming it, by beginning to act as if it were so, and then by experience finding out its trueness.

". . . the kingdom of God is at hand . . ." is a statement of inner realization. A man has shifted his focal point of heaven from a distant future to the "eternal now." He has become the recipient of "the whole creation travailing and groaning for the revealing of the sons of God"; and the "sons of God" are those who claim and experience identification and union with God.

To repent means to change direction—to change direction of thought, to change direction of expectancy, and to change direction of acceptance.

The difference this makes is illustrated by the gospel stories of people bringing the sick to Jesus for healing—*after the sun had set on the sabbath*. According to Jewish law and tradition it was unlawful to heal on the sabbath, with few exceptions. Because of this teaching and the people's accepting belief in it, people waited until the sabbath had officially come to an end before bringing the sick to Jesus for healing. One wonders how many people suffered untold agony and pain, needlessly? How many minds snapped and men and women became insane or had nervous breakdowns, needlessly? And how many people died, needlessly? All because of their *belief*.

But that was not true of everyone. There was the man with the withered hand in the synagogue on the sabbath day. The doctors of the law protested that the sabbath was not for healing; Jesus disagreed with them and commanded the man to stretch out his hand. The decision rested entirely with the man at that moment. Dare he go against the counsel of the scribes and priests? Dare he find the courage to defy the social and religious culture of his time? Jesus, in the truth of God, could stand there and command, and He could offer help, but only the man himself could make the decision. This man stretched forth his hand, and it was made like new. One has to admire, perhaps, the desperation of the cripple, and the courageous battle he fought within his own mind—and won!

Even in the time of Jesus those who believed in a present-tense Kingdom of God were in the minority. Most people lived lives waiting for "the setting of the sun." God was not limited by the sabbath. Thoughts and beliefs and traditions prevented God from expressing His eternal nature which is available to everyone at any time.

That is why the matter of *believing* is so vitally important. Belief opens or closes the windows of possibilities within us. If someone tells me that he will give me a book at three o'clock in the afternoon, my believing will determine whether or not I will get that book. On the assumption that the man is telling the truth, my belief makes the expression of that possibility possible. If I refuse to believe it, I miss the expression of reality. In missing it I have not changed the truth of it. I have simply prevented the channels of expression from entering my personal affairs.

Many people have never written a book, painted a picture, gone to college, married, or found contentment because they did not believe it was possible. Possibilities are not made less real by their unbelief; they are merely prevented from entering people's lives.

One might say, "But what if it isn't true? What if the man will not give me the book?" Then we naturally will not get the book. But if one's life is to be governed by the possibilities of a thing *not happening,* we will not try anything. To be governed by the fear of failure is to be ruled by smallness of spirit, never experiencing new discoveries nor living with great expectations.

One is reminded of the story often told about Thomas Edison. It is said that a woman came to him after he had told of the 1500 times he had failed in his experiments to invent the electric-light bulb. She said something like this to Mr. Edison: "Wasn't it awful that you had to fail all those times." His reply was classic and indicative of the belief that drove him on, "Madam, I have never failed. I simply learned 1500 ways that it would not work."

Life is a learning process if it is anything at all, and the person who is afraid of failing is beaten. He will never thrill to the fertile riches of human possibility. He is not even beaten before he begins because he will never begin. Learning is as much finding out what is not right as what is right. Life is discovery, and the only way to prevent the wonders of discovery is not to believe it is possible for you.

Belief is life itself. It drives the scientist to search for facts that are hidden. It keeps the artist striving after new forms. It keeps people seeking after something in their lives that is not yet fact. Belief is an instinctive knowing that draws people to discoveries that are not yet known. Belief is the subconscious awareness that there is an answer to whatever it is we are seeking. It is common to all aspects of living. It is an unconscious knowing that teases the conscious mind to try and to attempt.

So when Jesus told us to repent and believe the good news, He cast expectancies and attitudes on the side of God manifesting in the here and now, as well as in the hereafter. The scribes and the Pharisees also believed, but they believed in something that would happen in some indefinable future. Jesus said, "Now!" The saints and sages of all ages have said, "Now!" The wisdom of scripture says, "Now is the acceptable time."

When we say, "Our Father which art in heaven . . . ," it involves so much more than words. We can almost feel the awesome thrill of living inside the very mind and nature of Jesus of Nazareth. Basic to all His relationships He claims identification and union with God, expressed in and through all of life, and recognizes Himself as enveloped in that wholeness, inseparable and at one-ment.

When one enters, even remotely, into such an awareness, it is as if he were the vision of Isaiah all over again.

"In the year that king Uzziah died I saw also the Lord sitting upon a throne, high and lifted up, and his train filled the temple. Above it stood the seraphims: each one had six wings; with twain he covered his face, and with twain he covered his feet, and with twain he did fly. And one cried unto another, and said, Holy, holy, holy, is the Lord of hosts: the whole earth is full of his glory. And the posts of the door moved at the voice of him that cried, and the house was filled with smoke. Then said I, Woe is me! for I am undone; because I am a man of unclean lips, and I dwell in the midst of a people of unclean lips: for mine eyes have seen the King, the Lord of hosts" (6:1-5).

Remember the words of the heavenly beings, *that the whole earth is full of His glory*. Isaiah had seen creation stripped of the obscurity that hides the glory of God. Something of this sort also happened to the servant of the prophet Elijah when his eyes were opened and he saw the hillsides peopled by the heavenly hosts. When such an experience happens, one truly knows that the earth is the Lord's and that all creation is pregnant with the glory *that is God*. Psalm 148 also recognizes the saturation of God in all creation when the moon and the stars, the waters and the sea monsters, the fire and the hail, the snow and the frost, the trees and the cattle, and rulers and maidens and children are commanded to "praise the Lord!"

Such an experience is awesomely fearful. There are some sights, whether to the outer eyes or to the inward vision, that shake one by the very enormity of splendor. The human being reels from kaleidoscopic greatness and wonder and magnificence that is too great for the body and mind to endure for long. We too can only emulate the heavenly beings by saying, "Holy, holy, holy. . . ." There is no coercion in this form of worship. It is an unconscious, spontaneous outpouring of the human soul in symphony with a universe lost in the womb of God. We could no more stop such praise than we could cease life. When this happens we can really say we are "in Christ," and "Christ is in God," and all is in One, and One is in all.

But the story of Isaiah does not end with the splendor and the awe. In his awe about seeing something too glorious for human eyes to see, one of the heavenly beings flies to him with a hot coal and touches his lips, saying, "Behold, this has touched your lips; your guilt is taken away, and your sin forgiven" (6:7, RSV). Your sin is forgiven! What is sin? Separation! Separation between man and God is ended; the gulf is bridged. In such a state, what else is one to say to the voice of God in creation that is always yearning, "Whom shall I send, and who will go for us?" except, "Here am I; send me" (Isaiah 6:8).

One who has seen this is no more able to keep it to himself than he can refuse to be himself. The attempt has to be made even though the natural and normal man, adjusted to realization on a lower level of consciousness, will not comprehend nor understand. The new creature "in Christ" and "in God" will have a difficult time explaining what he is talking about. Words can be used, and they are used, but ultimately the only message that gets across is the quality of one's life.

How often we say about our deepest awarenesses, "Oh, if I could only put it into words!" If only, indeed! But we all know when something has happened to change a person's life. We see it in his eyes, in his facial expression, in a new dependability and yet an independence, in a new kindness, in a new patience, and in a new poise. We know from this that he is a "new creature." We may not be able to understand his explanation of what has happened, and his explanation may even seem irrational and illogical, but we cannot evade the fact of his personality and his adjustment and reaction to life. Because of the life, we will accept the words. However, words without a commensurate expression in living have no effect upon us at all.

Dwight L. Moody told a story about his boyhood that illustrates this perfectly. When he moved into a new neighborhood, the other children told him about a man who gave a dime to each new member of the neighborhood. Moody, like any boy, sought out the man. He got his dime, but he got more too. The man placed his hand on his head. It is said that Moody never lost the touch of that hand for the rest of his life. Somebody, some unknown man of God, blessed a little boy. His life was his message. And who is to say how much that had to do in eventually producing the man who became the greatest evangelist in his time?

People are stories incarnate! Words are minor factors. A woman told me that the memory that means more to her than anything else is that of her mother sitting on the steps of her home with her when she was a little girl, quietly, in the tenderness of love and acceptance. Her mother *was something*. Whatever words she remembers are of value only because they express the story incarnate that was her mother.

I remember a Sunday school teacher I had in Ireland. I cannot remember a word he said to me, but I remember the man. I wanted to be like him, and because I wanted to be like him I wanted to belong to his God. At that age I am sure I would have understood very little of his explanation, but he was his own explanation. He himself was all I needed to know, and whatever it was he had given his life to was what I wanted to give my life to. I am notorious for forgetting names, but I remember that man's name. It was Billy Beggs. I am sure he had no idea that he made much of an impression on me, but then how much do any of us know about those we have influenced?

Here then is the recognition and identification, and the being lost in Christ, and the results of it, that are included in the words ". . . which art in heaven."

We have but slightly explored the inherent possibilities in these words. More important than the words is the attitude. More important than the attitude is the total life and its adjustment to the entire cosmos, and ultimately to the God of the cosmos—"Our Father which art in heaven." This is intimate relationship in the most personal way. In this relationship the personal and the impersonal are swallowed up in a newness of life that is more subjectively personal than we formerly thought of as being personal. Every vibration and breath of the universe (of God Himself) becomes the body and mind extension of ourselves, and we lose ourselves in a perfect knowing that we are "lost in God."

2

Hallowed Be Thy Name

ALLOWED be thy name" follows most naturally. What else could one say, really?

Hallowed (holy, blessed, all praise, reverence, wholeness) is thy name. The "name" used in this manner refers to the nature, the intrinsic essence or being of the One referred to. The name is the verbal designation of the inward nature or spirit.

In ancient times children were given a name after the hopes that the parents had for them, or else a child was named after some event or experience that brought forth the child.

Samuel was named as he was because his mother had asked God for him, and the name means "God asked." What such a name must have meant to Hannah and to her son in later years can only be surmised. She must have told him why she gave him his name. Or maybe the old priest who ministered to Hannah in her sorrow when she went to the altar to ask God for a man-child told the boy about the incident and how he came to be named. At any rate, in Hannah's mind there could be no question—God had sent her child.

Every time that Hannah, and later on Samuel himself, used his name it was a reminder that he was God's child and God's man. He had a purpose in life, for if he was the result of prayer and supplication rather than human will, then God had a plan for him.

Surely the constant hearing of his name tended to push Samuel in the direction of his mother's promise to God: ". . . I will give him unto the Lord all the days of his life . . ." (I Samuel 1:11). Each time the name would be uttered it would be one more spiritual impress into the dream and into the intention. Is it any wonder that a little boy who knew he was "God asked" and also "God promised" would turn into a man of special importance?

As the "name" in Hebrew history referred to the intrinsic nature of the person, it was only natural that when the nature changed the name would also be changed. Thus we have the story of Jacob who became Israel.

With his mother's cooperation he robbed his brother Esau of his birthright. Esau threatened, "The days of mourning for my father are approaching; then I will kill my brother Jacob" (Genesis 27:41, RSV). The news of this threat was given to their mother Rebekah, and at her insistence Jacob fled to his mother's country and to her brother. There Jacob became rich and married. When he decided to return home, after many years, he was afraid and prayed, "Deliver me, I pray thee, from the hand of my brother, from the hand of Esau: for I fear him, lest he will come and smite me, and the mother with the children" (Genesis 32:11).

Jacob's day of reckoning drew near, and his cleverness and wit failed him. Or, perhaps a man comes to the end of guile and wants to make amends and begin a new life in honesty and honor. Jacob wrestled all night with an angel before he was to face his brother Esau. When the angel told him to let him go as the dawn was breaking, Jacob refused and clung to the angel for his blessing. He was asked his name and replied, "Jacob." He was then told, "Your name shall no more be called Jacob, but Israel, for you have striven with God and with men, and have prevailed" (Genesis 32:28, RSV).

He had been called "Jacob" because at his birth he was born after his twin brother Esau and in the process of birth held on to Esau's heel. Perhaps this is indicative of his later feeling of inferiority and weakness in the presence of the more masculine Esau. It might account for his recourse to cleverness and guile in order to compete with him.

Regardless of the reasons for Jacob's character, the change in his nature resulted in the change of his name to "Israel" ("he who strives with God and prevails").

In some ways it is regrettable that the ancient custom of name-giving has vanished. Today a name means almost nothing, but it is interesting to speculate on the results if children today were named either according to the dreams and hopes of the parents, or according to some special event or manner of their birth.

In the Lord's Prayer, "thy name" has rich meaning. The history of Israel is reviewed in a phrase that brings to mind stories of faithful patriarchs, judges, kings, and prophets, all of them well known to a Hebrew in Jesus' time. Such a Hebrew would remember that God had not judged his people "according to their transgressions," but innumerable times had not remembered their unfaithfulness. He would remember Moses and the leading of the children of Israel out of slavery into the Promised Land, and the return from captivity in Babylon. His imagination would be quickened by the cloud that led the nation by day, and the pillar of fire by night, the giving of the Ten Commandments, special protection in wars and raids by wandering tribes and neighboring nations, Gideon and his gallant band, David the young shepherd-lad who became a mighty king, the prophets who stung the conscience of a nation into practicing justice, and the lovely lesson of Ruth—in short the history of a nation with a long and special relationship with the living and loving God. His nation was a chosen people, chosen by God Himself, to have a special mission to the whole world. His entire culture was God-centered.

When Jesus said, "Hallowed by thy name," the whole panorama of His people, of which He was a part, must have flashed into His mind. And as it did, and as He remembered the love and longing and tenderness of God, He knew that the nature of God was so wonderful that God was holy beyond words, that God was worthy of praise beyond measure, that there was no lacking in His abundance, no weakening in His faithfulness, and no describing His glory.

Like the Psalmist, one could only say, "O Lord our Lord, how excellent is thy name in all the earth!" (Psalms 8:1). Psalm 145 opens with: "I will extol thee, my God, O king; and I will bless thy name for ever and ever. Every day I will bless thee; and I will praise thy name for ever and ever. Great is the Lord, and greatly to be praised; and his greatness is unsearchable." This is the Hebrew picture and understanding of "the name of the Lord."

However, a man's understanding of the nature of God is not limited to historical considerations. He comes to a personal conception and attitude that goes beyond the territory of the past. He makes a synthesis of the past and of his own experiences to come to something that is uniquely his own.

We find much in the gospels concerning Jesus' own attitudes and ideas about God. At the very beginning of the Lord's Prayer the word of identification is "Father," and it reminds us that He once said, ". . . call no man your father on earth, for you have one Father, who is in heaven" (Matthew 23:9, RSV). Through a patriarchal society we step inside the mind of Jesus when He chose to use this word. The entire life of the family revolved around the father. Genealogies were traced through the father; the family was utterly dependent upon the father for everything: their protection depended upon the father; inheritance came through the father; food and the meeting of all physical needs was the job of the father. The father held a very special place, so much so that it is difficult for us to imagine his importance in terms of today's society. In the United States today, where women work and compete on equal terms with men in every area of life, and where women can inherit and be financially and socially independent, it is well-nigh impossible to appreciate the role of the father in distant times. In our imagination we can sense, however, what the word must have meant to Jesus.

However, the dominion, provision, and protection of God was not limited, in Jesus' mind, to the human being. It included nature as well. He was creation's Father as well as the Father of men and women.

"Consider the lilies of the field," He said, ". . . they toil not, neither do they spin: . . . if God so clothe the grass of the field, which to day is, and to morrow is cast into the oven, shall he not much more clothe you . . . ?" (Matthew 6:28, 30).

Again He said, "Look at the birds of the air: they neither sow nor reap nor gather into barns, and yet your heavenly Father feeds them" (Matthew 6:26, RSV).

Jesus rebukes men and women by drawing their attention to nature, and tells them to emulate the faith and trust they see there. The thread of His reasoning is inescapable: in a right attitude and relationship with God, our needs are met as perfectly on the physical plane as they are on the spiritual. Here again we catch a glimpse of family life in Jesus' time. Apparently it was quite inconceivable to Jesus that a man would not give the same trust to God that he would give to his earthly father. At least this much trust was necessary.

In the well-loved passage about asking, seeking, and knocking, the rationale of Jesus runs from the particular to the universal, from the family relationship to the godly: "Ask, and it shall be given you; seek, and ye shall find; knock, and it shall be opened unto you. For every one that asketh receiveth; and he that seeketh findeth; and to him that knocketh it shall be opened. Or what man is there of you, whom if his son ask bread, will he give him a stone? Or if he ask a fish, will he give him a serpent? If ye then, being evil, know how to give good gifts unto your children, how much more shall your Father which is in heaven give good things to them that ask him?" (Matthew 7:7-11).

The same passage, as it is written in the Gospel of Luke (11:13), ends with a slightly different slant.

"If ye then, being evil, know how to give good gifts unto your children: how much more shall your heavenly Father give the Holy Spirit to them that ask him?"

One account says that the heavenly Father will give good things, and the other says that He will give the Holy Spirit (the spirit or nature of God Himself).

The picture we get here of the nature (or the name) of God is sharply different from a picture we get from some people today who make of God not something better than man, but something infinitely worse. Some of the pictures depict such awful vengeance and torture that they make Adolf Hitler quite attractive by comparison. It was not so with the picture of God drawn by Jesus. The Heavenly Father presented by Jesus is not infinitely worse than man, but infinitely more provident, more kind, more healing and forgiving.

In the asking, seeking, and knocking account, the basic conclusion we can draw is that the *right spirit* and *the right things* are closely related to each other, if not actually two faces of the same coin. The right spirit, the proper relationship of man and God based on loving trust, the right attitude between God and man in love and attraction, result in the right things. The things follow as naturally as a flower unfolds in the right climate. The channel through which the right things flow to us is over the bridge of spirit, relationship and attitude.

Jesus maintained this relationship of Father and Son in times of extreme crisis. After He had upbraided the cities of His time for their refusal to understand and accept what He lived and taught, after seeing His mission (from every human point of view) on the brink of failure, He once again knew that His life and affairs were in the hands of God; and God as Sire, Provider, wise Counselor, infinite in wisdom, purposeful, in whom all things and relationships reside, is still "Head of the family" and "knows best."

"At that time Jesus answered . . . , I thank thee, O Father, Lord of heaven and earth, because thou hast hid these things from the wise and prudent [understanding], and hast revealed them unto babes. Even so, Father: for so it seemed good in thy sight" (Matthew 11:25).

The nature of God, to Jesus, was such as to elicit absolute trust even when, to the child's outer sight and understanding, things seemed to be falling apart.

We understand much of the inner sight and understanding and attitudes of Jesus from His very actions as well as from His words. As he was the Word (*Logus*) incarnate, God in human form—or perhaps all we can conceive of God in human nature —then His words have meaning only as they are interpreted in His actions. He not only talked about healing the body; He performed it. His actions revealed the intent and illustrated the application of the things He said.

Thus we find Him stilling the winds, calming the waters of the Sea of Galilee, providing food for the multitudes, restoring sick bodies and warped minds, freeing men from wrong ideas and giving hope to the hopeless.

There is no reference to Jesus ever even hinting that the disability of a person came from God or was the intention of God. There is the story of the woman who was bent over, crippled, for eighteen years. The scribes and the Pharisees were waiting to see if He would attempt to heal the woman on the sabbath. In their minds, and by their words, the sabbath was holy—it belonged to God. Yet the expression of a day holy to God was a step and an application they quite evidently could not take. It is Jesus who took the step and made the application: ". . . ought not this . . . daughter of Abraham whom Satan bound for eighteen years, be loosed from this bond on the sabbath . . . ?" (Luke 13:16, RSV).

The reasoning of Jesus is direct and reveals something of Himself. If God were truly worshiped on the sabbath, if God really had the opportunity to express Himself more fully on this day than on other days, then miracles ought to be more common and the ills of men and women ought to be more readily cured.

If tradition and social custom came into conflict with the name of God, Jesus did not hesitate. When the tax collector, Matthew, gave a party and invited Jesus to come and meet his friends, He did so. The Pharisees certainly did not think that looked like the conduct of a man of God. The answer of Jesus was pointed: "Those who are well have no need of a physician, but those who are sick. Go and learn what this means, 'I desire mercy, and not sacrifice.' For I came not to call the righteous, but sinners" (Matthew 9:12-13, RSV).

Too often our actions are determined by tradition, and by social and religious habits, instead of by the "name" of God.

When ritual or tradition take the place of right relationship, when they become a substitute for personal responsibility and sensitivity; they must always be rejected and condemned. Thus we have such a statement as "It is better to obey than to offer sacrifice."

The nature of God, as understood by Jesus and lived by Him, is contained in the word "love," and the understanding of what He meant by love has to be interpreted by His actions and by His life.

He approved the summation of the law and the prophets, as spoken by a lawyer who said, ". . . thou shalt love the Lord thy God with all thy heart, . . . and . . . mind, and . . . strength: . . . And the second is like, namely this, Thou shalt love they neighbour as thyself" (Mark 12:30-31).

He said, "A new commandment I give to you, that you love one another; even as I have loved you, . . . By this all men will know that you are my disciples, if you have love for one another" (John 13:34-35, RSV).

The key to what Jesus means by love is in the phrase, ". . . even as I have loved you, that you love one another." His kind of love, as revealed in His actions and also in His words, is most definitely not the sentimental by-product that we often associate with it today.

If Jesus was the incarnation of the nature or the name of God, then His actions are the expression of love in all His relationships. If this is true, then He illustrated love as much in the whipping incident in the temple as He did when He invited the little children to come to Him and blessed them. He was as much the expression of the love of God, or the love which *is* God, when He commended Peter as when He rebuked him with "Get thee behind me, Satan . . ." (Matthew 16:23). He was just as much the expression of the "name" of God when He called the scribes and Pharisees a "generation of vipers" (Matthew 3:7) and "whited sepulchres" (Matthew 23:27) as He was when He said the immortal words, "Let not your heart be troubled . . ." (John 14:1).

This kind of love has steel in it. It is not vapid. It has purpose. It has discipline and a certain amount of ruthlessness. It is the kind of love that made Jesus publicly rebuke His family and tell the crowd that His family were those who did the will of God. No human relationship could stand in its way, nor would Jesus permit it to do so.

In the parable of the marriage feast the invited guests made all kinds of excuses not to attend. The servants were then sent out into the highways and byways to get people to come to the feast. The point is, the wedding feast was held on schedule! In other words, God's will will be done. Man's acceptance or rejection of it does not compromise the nature of God nor the intention of God, and true love does not compromise itself simply because the recipient of it happens to be a friend.

How horrible it would be if such a thing were possible! Then it would inevitably mean that God would be limited to the image and nature of man rather than man being transformed into the image of God. In that kind of an upside-down world, life would indeed be hopelessly awful. Jesus invited and commanded the disciples to follow Him; He did not follow them. By His example He did not bend and yield to the world of expediency. When His disciples dreamed that He would rule an earthly kingdom, He disappointed them; and He refused when the crowd wanted to make Him a king. He was true to His mission and to the nature that came from God.

We see no difference in His behavior and His words when events were unfolding according to His wishes than when they were appallingly in opposition to His efforts. He was stalwart, dependable, responsible, and predictable. Circumstances could not make Him deviate.

In the mind of Jesus the personal immanence of God and the nonpersonal law of God are lost in each other. One of the cruelties of human relationships is to see a child or an adult who does not know the sureness of discipline. Where there are rules and laws to live by, standards of conduct and behavior—a time to go to bed, a time to eat, a way to dress for certain occasions, demands of responsibility—there is security and there is love. The one without such patterns of conduct feels unwanted and unnecessary. Life has little direction or meaning. It results in all sorts of mental and emotional aberrations.

There is a wonderful story about those who mutinied on the *H.M.S. Bounty.* When they came to the islands where they settled—a Pacific paradise to their eyes and to their way of thinking—they were sure they had attained heaven on earth. There were no rules to live by. They were free from the commands of their officers, there were no police to enforce laws, and there were no courts to pass judgment and penalty upon them. This, they thought, was the dream of their lives come true.

As time went by they discovered something they had not bargained for. Family relationships were impossible. What anyone wanted, he took, if he had the strength or will to do so. No one's wife or mate was safe. No husband could be trusted. Property was for the asking, or rather the taking. Might was right. Whatever suited one's momentary whim was unrestrained. Before long, fear ruled the island; fear not only of others, but of oneself. No one could be trusted, not even the one wanting to find trust. What they had thought of as heaven on earth became hell on earth.

Then, it is said, someone remembered that they had had a Bible on the ship. They went back and found it. They read it greedily in order to learn how to live, in order to find security, in order to know the rules, and the God of the rules. Trust once more became possible, and with it a return to mental, emotional, and physical balance.

Jesus did not teach license, but He did teach liberty, and liberty was to be found in the discipline of rules. He explained it in this way: "As the Father has loved me, so have I loved you; abide in my love" (John 15:9, RSV).

How?

"If you keep my commandments, you will abide in my love, just as I have kept my Father's commandments and abide in his love" (v. 10).

And what will be the result of this sort of duty and commandment?

"These things I have spoken to you, that my joy may be in you, and that your joy may be full" (v. 11).

The purpose of the nature of God (and therefore of life) is not to frustrate the expression and attainment of man's instinctive nature. It is to fulfill it, and to enable him to achieve what his nature demands: fulfillment, contentment, achievement, and joy. But achievement does not come from ignoring the manner in which our law-abiding universe is built. Rules are there to *facilitate* the expression of God's nature and to bring a man's life into harmony with the spirit and laws of life. They are put there to make it possible for the good things of life to be man's.

Jesus saw this as illustrated in the human family headed by a good father. A good father disciplines not to hurt but to help, not to frustrate but to release, not to imprison but to set free, not to withhold but to make it possible to give, not to produce fear but to produce love, and not to inhibit the personality but to release it.

A father thought he was being kind to his son by not insisting upon anything. The boy could study when he wanted to, he could look at television when he wanted to, he could make his own decisions about clothing and companions, and he could decide for himself what he wanted to be. There was as little guidance as possible. The father thought he was treating the son like a man, and that his son would appreciate it. For a while he did, and then one day, in sheer miserableness, the son came to his father and said something like this: "I wish there were something you wanted me to do—that you made me do. It just seems that I am not needed for anything."

After a long and open discussion, they both decided they had been wrong; they needed each other. The father needed to know what it meant to be needed by his son, and the son needed to know that his father cared enough about him to give him the guidance and direction he was too young to handle by himself.

True love does not confiscate the rules of life, but makes a fine adjustment to them. Just as all nature is subject to the laws of life, and every element of nature succeeds which comes into cooperation with them, so it is with man. When a man comes into conformity with the nature of God, the "name" of God, he finds his personality blossoming into a wholeness that in rebellion to the nature of God (or, the laws of life) is impossible. Life takes on direction instead of aimless expediency; the restlessness of tension gives way to contentment; the accidental appearance of much of life gives way to pattern and form even if we cannot be precise about the meaning of each little incident; and a man finds an inner appreciation of his own personal worth. This regime leads to a reverence for all life—and the God of all life—that is not possible in any other way.

So when Jesus' mind expresses itself in the words, "Hallowed be thy name," it means that wholeness is the nature of God. Man is instinctively or intuitively aware of this perfection and reaches for it; he is attracted by it and tends in the direction of it. One does not have to be aware of the word *God*. The word itself is not important. The reality of our nature (made in the image and likeness of God) that apprehends it is the important thing. God has many names, even in the Bible. There are such descriptive names as Counselor, King, Shepherd, Rock, Shield, Father, High Tower, Strong Arm, and many, many others. Someone has said there are about two hundred names for God in the Bible. The moment one begins to splinter the absolute wholeness which is God, the number of splinters are as infinite as the complete is infinite. The important and self-revealing thing is that our nature is aware of God and in fact demands Him. Apparently we would build a god if there were none. Saint Augustine put it in these words: "Thou hast made us for thyself and our souls are restless until they find their rest in thee." Dr. Glenn Clark used to say that we are all angels with amnesia and it often takes a knock on the head to awaken us to who we really are.

The evidence for a directive intelligence is demonstrated in any historical study of science. We may not always be sure of the goal of nature, but that it is changing, has changed, and seems to be in no mood to cease changing, is inescapable. The changing forms of life, as evidenced by any study of biology, are striking. Nature is not static. Some forms of life have ceased to exist. We can find fossils which indicate species that are no longer here. We can witness that those forms of life which were most adaptable to changing climate and environment have been the ones to continue to inhabit the earth. Species such as the sabre-toothed tiger, mastodons, and other creatures that ruled supreme in past ages are no longer with us. We find animal life today that is all but extinct. Life is moving; it is growing or expanding and in a state of flux.

Astronomers tell us that the universe is expanding. Galaxies are receding from each other at enormous rates of speed. The astronomers tell us that they witnessed the birth and death of stars and galaxies. They tell us that creation is not something that happened once at the beginning of time and then ceased, but that it is a continuing process.

Certainly life today is more abundant than at any time in past history. In spite of the fact that many today are in hunger and need, we are told that if man could learn to live on this earth in harmony and peace there would be no mouth wanting for food, no body wanting for clothing, and no tongue dry with thirst. As far as we know, there has never been a time in history when the population of the world was as great as it is now; and even with this population explosion we are capable of feeding the world. With scientific progress we seem to be on the verge of an abundance unimagined in history—if we can keep from destroying ourselves.

The inherent abundance of the earth is simply amazing. One man has said that if we consider only the amount of food consumed by the birds of the air every day, and how much it would cost if we had to purchase it, the figure is simply staggering. No country in the world has that kind of money. Yet, the small part of God expressed in what we call nature feeds them every day. When one thinks about it, he cannot but stand in awe of the abundance all about us waiting to be released for the benefit of all earth's creatures.

One of the attributes of the "name" or nature of God is this tremendous abundance. Abundance is not limited to food. Food is but one of the many avenues through which the abundant nature of God is made known to us. There are all kinds of other expressions. Man's capacities for abundance in love, inventiveness, creative expression in the arts, and possibilities of thinking in all areas are limitless. An expression which caused many to smile during World War II was that we could do the possible right away and that the impossible would take but a little longer. We are told today that not even our foremost scientists can predict what the near future holds in inventiveness and unthought-of possibilities of the mind and nature.

Abundance is all about us, pressing in on us, almost groaning for expression and manifestation. I once heard Norman Vincent Peale preach a sermon. I forget the title of it, but at one point he was talking about the words of Jesus: "I am come that they might have life, and that they might have it more abundantly" (John 10:10). In trying to explain it in a different way Dr. Peale said, "I am come that they might have life—lots of it, lots of it!"

"Hallowed be thy name" might well be paraphrased as "Wholeness, completeness, abundance, love, wisdom is the nature of Thy being."

We must approach this, *not* from the standpoint that God *can be* abundant, or that God *can* permit us to be abundant, like a tool to be used at one's whim or will and then discarded as he sees fit. It is not that at all. It is the very nature of God. Rather, it *is* the nature of God, just as love *is* the nature of God, health and healing and wholeness are the nature of God, and as the Apostle Paul says, he must be true to his own nature.

Hallowed be thy name! This is realization, a coming into a right relationship with God and the expression of Him in His creation, His manifest body in the universe, affirming something we instinctively know, and confirming something our nature demands. The only responsible reaction is a natural and spontaneous act of worship expressed in reverence and love and discipline and obedience to such a "name."

3

Thy Kingdom Come

ONE cannot catch a glimpse of heaven, the revealing of God's nature (or "name"), without saying and wanting and yearning and demanding, "Thy Kingdom *come!*"

In the Sermon on the Mount, Jesus tells us to seek first God and His Kingdom and righteousness, and all the things we desire will be ours as well. In another place He says that it is the Father's *good pleasure* to give us the Kingdom. God's intention is to have it happen; *we* prevent it by unbelief, wrong thinking, false goals, warped attitudes, and weak expectancies. God's nature and purpose in creation, and His expressive intent in life, is to manifest this perfection whenever it is permitted.

Experts tell us that in human history there is a common myth and story about a "Coming One." It is not limited to the Judeo-Christian tradition; it is universal. Primitive man believed that God was separated from His creation and from man himself. Man sensed, or knew, that community with God was the answer to his problems. This knowing was an untaught and natural knowledge within himself. There were no schools or churches to teach primitive man about God. The only explanation for such awareness is that the Creator placed it there in the very fibers of man's nature.

Man's unconscious knowing took two forms of searching to substantiate it consciously. One method was the investigation of nature (and himself as part of nature). This is the method of science. Here is man's basic belief that if he can know enough about nature—discovering the laws that govern nature, studying how nature works and is related, investigating the life and rationale of all that he sees, touches, smells, feels, tastes, and hears —he can then come into a proper relationship with it and use it for his own ends of abundance, protection, power, health, and everything else the mind and heart desires. In science, man is looking for the secret of life hidden in everything about him. The methodology is investigation and the cataloguing of facts to search out patterns and formulate theories of meaning. In most cases the word "God" is not used. Other words are perhaps preferable to the researcher, such as "truth," "reality," "nature," "beauty," "existence," and many others. Many times these words are printed with capital letters which indicates that there is a sensing of something beyond what meets the eye.

The other method in the history of man's search for relatedness is religion. It is a more direct approach to the mystery of life. Man has always sensed a "something" behind and beyond what meets the human eye. His reasoning seems to be that "something" had to make all that he sees, the world "and they that dwell therein." He believes that if he can come into a right relationship with Him who made it all, if he can gain the favor of God, then his troubles will be over and he can enter into living a life free from fear, poverty, ignorance, ugliness, and cruelty.

Put a cow in a field and, from what we know, she is content to exist. Whatever intelligence she has, as far as we know, is dictated by the primary urges for food, survival, and procreation. The cow is content to be a cow. Put a man in that same field and, while he may be driven by the same basic urges, he is also driven by much more. Before long he will begin wondering where he came from, what he is doing there, what is the meaning or purpose of himself, where he is going, what causes the seasons, and many other thoughts. Descartes once wrote, "I think, therefore I am." Thinking is the chief occupation of the human being. The quality of his thinking differentiates him from all other forms of life.

Before long, man has many ideas and theories about himself and the whole of life. Soon he has a system of thought about the nature of the Being who is behind all creation and responsible for it. In fact, one of the inescapable facts of history is man's obsession with God. Wherever one goes in his study of history, the urge to find meaning, and to worship, is universal. In the primitive mind the search for this elusive reality seemed his chief occupation. We soon find altars to the rivers, the trees, the stars, the seasons of the year, the processes of nature, and when he had exhausted the possibilities of his imagination he still had the feeling that there was more, something he had not embraced, and so, he then made an altar to "The Unknown God."

The reason for his search, his altars, and his rites was to find community with a distant God separated from His creation, to "bring Him down" and gain His favor. Man gave God the best that he knew in order to win His favor and gain His help. The greatest thing he could think of was life itself, so he killed and sacrificed to his gods what was most loved by him. Animals were sacrificed with the intention of making a worthy gift to God. Then man went further; he sacrificed his own kind. In ancient Hebrew lands, and also in the surrounding countries, it was common to sacrifice the firstborn male of any creature. The male in men or animals was of more importance in the primitive mind than the female. Thus we have the story in the Bible of Abraham on the brink of sacrificing his son. It must have been one of the great moments in history when he realized that this was not pleasing to God (not in community with truth and reality).

Great as that was, it was still a long way to where man was told to offer "sacrifices" of joy, praise, thanksgiving, and the like. The distance from the primitive conception of blood sacrifice to praise and thanksgiving is very great.

The way to bring God down (as the primitives would put it), or to come into community with God, gradually changed from the idea of sacrifice to living in a manner ethically pleasing to a higher conception of God. The prophets exposed and condemned injustice wherever they found it. What would please God was not ritual, calendar seasons, fasts, and the like, but rather a life lived personally and socially in a manner that would reflect the perfect character of God Himself.

Isaiah 58 is a classic example of this sort of thinking (and how far it is removed from the primitive idea of killing!) that God is pleased and "comes down" only when man lives in a manner that is "acceptable" to Him. In this great chapter the people ask (v. 3, RSV):

Why have we fasted, and thou seest it not? Why have we humbled ourselves, and thou takest no knowledge of it?

The answer follows immediately (vv. 4-5, RSV):

> Behold, you fast only to quarrel and to fight and to hit with the wicked fist. Fasting like yours this day will not make your voice to be heard on high. . . . Will you call this a fast, and a day acceptable to the Lord?

Then the writer specifically depicts what is "acceptable" to God, the kind of conduct that will make God near and will "bring Him down" (vv. 6-7, RSV):

> Is not this the fast that I choose: to loose the bonds of wickedness, to undo the thongs of the yoke, to let the oppressed go free, and to break every yoke? Is it not to share your bread with the hungry, and bring the homeless poor into your house; when you see the naked, to cover him, and not to hide yourself from your own flesh?

What will be the result of all this? What is the purpose of it all? Why do it (v. 8, RSV)?

> Then shall your light break forth like the dawn, and your healing shall spring up speedily; your righteousness shall go before you, the glory of the Lord shall be your rear guard. Then shall you call, and the Lord will answer; you shall cry, and he will say, Here I am.

That which is pleasing to God is that which is in harmony with His nature, and that which is the expression of His nature in human affairs. It is this which is "acceptable" to Him. This is what the prophets meant by bringing in "the acceptable year of the Lord."

We have the same idea and insight in chapter 61 of Isaiah. "God with us" or "God in us" results in certain desires and the expression of those desires in behavior.

"The Spirit of the Lord God is upon me . . ." (61:1, RSV) How do I know?

> . . . because the Lord has anointed me to bring good tidings to the afflicted; he has sent me to bind up the brokenhearted, to proclaim liberty to the captives, and the opening of the prison to those who are bound; to proclaim the year of the Lord's favor, and the day of vengeance of our God; to comfort all who mourn; to grant to those who mourn in Zion—to give them a garland

instead of ashes, the oil of gladness instead of mourning, the mantle of praise instead of a faint spirit; that they may be called oaks of righteousness, the planting of the Lord, that he may be glorified (61:1-3, RSV).

To glorify God, to worship in an acceptable manner, to have God express Himself in a person, is to do all these things; and the doing of all these things is the expression of God's Kingdom on earth.

Jesus of Nazareth could not express His idea of God's Kingdom and union with God any better than to quote from this same prophet. When He entered the synagogue at Nazareth to announce His mission and the direction of His life, He opened the scroll of Isaiah and read: "The Spirit of the Lord is upon me, because he has anointed me to preach good news to the poor. He has sent me to proclaim release to the captives and recovering of sight to the blind, to set at liberty those who are oppressed, to proclaim the acceptable year of the Lord" (Luke 4:18-19, RSV).

The words were not new to the people in the synagogue. They had heard them many times, and they were always associated with the great prophet of the past. Perhaps there was a faint hope that it might happen again, that another prophet or man of God would come among them and bring God and His Kingdom near, but they were shocked when Jesus said, "Today this scripture has been fulfilled in your hearing" (v. 21, RSV).

The people murmured and said, "Is not this Joseph's son?" (v. 22, RSV). They did not accept Him. While people have an insatiable thirst for God's expression in their lives, the desire is usually projected to some obscure future date or event. There seems to be a reluctance about accepting the possibility or reality of it in the here and now.

At any rate there is little doubt but that in Jesus' mind the Kingdom of God and its expression in human society had very precise and definite results. In Matthew 25 He describes the judgment. The picture is revealing about His view of life on earth and purpose of it. He will say to some, "Come, O blessed of my Father, inherit the kingdom prepared for you from the foundation of the world; for I was hungry and you gave me food, I was thirsty and you gave me drink, I was a stranger and you welcomed me, I was naked and you clothed me, I was sick and you visited me, I was in prison and you came to me" (vv. 34-36, RSV). In the mind of Jesus, true worship of God was true service to mankind; and true service to man was coming into oneness with God.

Implied in all these ideas is the realization that the Kingdom has not totally come, or manifested itself completely, on earth and in the affairs of men. There would be no need to do all this if all people were well fed, clothed, free, treated justly and mercifully. There is a job to be done; therefore there is the desire and the affirmation in the Lord's Prayer, "Thy kingdom come." And, in that "come" there is a responsibility laid upon everyone who says it. Each has a job to do to bring it in, to extend the boundaries of God's reign and rule, to manifest the spirit and nature of perfection on earth.

One man has said, "Thy Kingdom come, and *let it begin with me*." One way of interpreting this may seem quite selfish, but there is another way to look at it. It indicates the willingness and intention of the individual to be the territory in which that Kingdom of perfection may express itself now, no matter whether or not anyone else in the world so chooses. It is an offering of one's body and personality for the use of that expression which is the Spirit of God.

If there is one emphasis in the life of Jesus that distinguishes Him from the Eastern religions, it is the emphasis that the material universe is not an illusion, not something to be shunned as evil in itself, and not something that one ought to reject as delusion or unimportant. When He sent out His disciples, two by two, He told them to preach the Good News of the Kingdom of God *and to heal the sick*. If the world and the people of the world were not real and worth doing something about, if there was not a world to be won that was worth winning, He would not have given those instructions to the disciples as they left on their mission.

I once flew to a distant city to have charge of a retreat. I arrived there tired and mentally depressed. Perhaps I had been working too hard for too long. Perhaps economic and political conditions left little to be content with or optimistic about. At any rate, I felt in no condition to be leading others in a search for reality and a deeper meaning for their lives. After I had checked into my hotel room I remember sitting on the side of the bed and thinking to myself, "If anybody needs a retreat, it is I. I doubt that anyone coming to the church tomorrow will be in more need."

As I sat there wondering what to do, my eyes fell on the Bible. I opened it idly and began thumbing through the pages. I came to the story of Jesus sending out the disciples two by two and the instructions He gave them. *Preach the Good News of the Kingdom of Heaven.* Then I thought, "Well, what else is there to talk about? What else *might* they have talked about?"

Politics could be one subject. There was enough of it in the Palestine of Jesus' time. There was enough political gossip and rumor and graft for many speeches, but His instructions were not to talk about that. Maybe people were as sick of politics as I was at that moment.

They could have talked about economic conditions. It was hard to make a living in those times. There was no social security to cushion the harsh demands of being out of a job. There was no fair-employment-practices law. Jesus did not tell His disciples to talk about economics and the problems of unemployment.

They might have talked about loose social conditions and the laxity of morals among those in positions of prestige and popularity. John the Baptist has been executed by a government official because he had publicly exposed such an incident. A dancing girl and her mother saw to that. But the disciples were not told to devote themselves to such things.

They were to keep their minds and their energies focused on one thing only—the Kingdom of God, the Good News of it —and to heal the sick. I got my direction right there and then for the retreat. What I had to say was on the right subject, and apparently did a lot of good.

What is the Good News of the Kingdom? The Kingdom of God? *It is here!* It is not a distant reality. We are so enmeshed in the tragedies and weaknesses of life that we take our eyes off this important fact. Jesus never did. God was the most important fact in His life, and so was the revealing of the nature of God in human affairs. They were both one and the same to Him. One could not have God without His expression, His realm, and His rule. The Kingdom of God, the fulfillment of the desires and dreams and wants and needs of every man, was not something that one had to wait for until he died, any more than he had to wait for God until he died.

It is within you. The Kingdom of God is not something exterior to oneself. It expresses in individual lives and in society as a whole through the channels of the human heart and soul and mind and body. In a sense the individual is the Kingdom of Heaven, even if he is not aware of it. It is not something imposed upon a person; it is something released within him.

Why do we want that which is beautiful? Why are we attracted by a beautiful flower, a color that lifts the spirits, a curve on a piece of paper which seems perfect, a piece of machinery that is "just right," a picture that makes us want to look at it the second time and the third time, or a harmony of sound that causes us to exclaim, "Isn't that beautiful?" One might answer, "But everyone does that." Of course, but why? Is there any logical reason why we could not have been created to love ugliness instead of beauty? None at all. All we can say is that we were not created that way.

Why does everyone seek after health and shy away from illness? Again, one might say, "But everyone does that." Of course, but why? There is no reason why we could not have been built to love ill health and disease, and to be attracted by pain. We might find this hard to believe because we are not used to such thoughts, but it could have been. When we find a person who is in love with sickness and delights in pain, we say he is mentally ill. There are people of that sort. When they delight to have pain inflicted upon themselves we call them masochists; and when they delight in inflicting pain upon others we call them sadists. We say they are perverted, their energies and goals have become turned about, upside-down, inside-out, and directed toward ends they were never intended for. They are sick.

Such perversions can be refined; they are not always as obvious as physical whipping. Once I attended a meeting high in the mountains of West Virginia. It was in a little tar-papered shack. The preacher held the listeners in terror for over an hour as she whipped them with *words* of an impending hell, the fall of brimstone that would burn but never consume, the inherent sinfulness of their nature that could only result in such a holocaust. Yes, there was the call to repent, and to repent, and to repent—and to beg forgiveness. From what I could learn, all those who were present were members of the little mountain sect and the service was normal for them. It was not long before people were literally screaming to God for mercy, and the time came when some were writhing on the floor in apparent agony as they continued to cry for mercy. The picture of God that must have been etched on the sensitive minds of the little children who were present can only be imagined.

After the meeting we met the preacher and some of her flock and told them we were at a nearby church-grounds for a week-long series of meetings, and we invited them to attend if they desired. A few days later I was speaking when I noticed three or four of them enter the room. They sat far in the back and listened. That day I was talking on the theme that "the love of God is broader than the reaches of men's minds."

A remarkable thing happened. These people became positively angry. It was reflected in their faces and the way they shook heads at each other. That was not the gospel to them! They had become so accustomed to verbal beratement, mental beatings, fear, and terror that they had come to enjoy it. It was not too long before they left the meeting. One wonders how they could enjoy heaven when they had habituated all their attitudes and feelings toward hell!

Why do we love freedom and liberty? These are not modern terms or conceptions. Peoples have fought for their freedom for as long as we have any recorded history, and we must assume that people were doing it before recorded history. There is something within the human breast that demands to be free. Even if a people have been in slavery for hundreds of years, the child that is recently born has the seed of freedom within him. This seed, sowed in his very nature, has been the fear of every dictator since the world began. It takes very little to make it stir and sprout.

The story of human history is also the story of the freeing of the human mind from ignorance and superstition. Knowledge is light to lighten the darkness of ignorance. It is no wonder that we used the name "Light" for God. The Gospel of John says that there is a "light" that "enlightens every man . . . coming into the world" (1:9, RSV), something within that demands that the darkness fly away.

A missionary in South America told a wonderful story about

electricity coming to a village. Before it came, night was a time of fear and uncertainty. People locked their doors and they would venture into the darkness only in an emergency. The cloak of darkness was the time for crime of every description. Then came electricity and the incandescent bulb. The entire village was lit up at night almost as much as it had been in the daytime. The outer light was marvelous, but what it did to people's minds and emotions was even more of a miracle. Fear and terror vanished, tensions melted away, and suspicion died. In comparison with how they lived before electricity and the light bulb, this was a miracle. This indeed was liberty. They were freed from ignorance, superstition, and fear.

Why do we seek abundance? There is no reason why we could not have been made for poverty and starvation. We simply were not made that way, and that is about all that can be said for it. The human belly is made to assimilate food; when food is denied, the body strives after it. We cannot be content and remain at rest when this function remains unfulfilled. Anyone who feeds a hungry mouth has manifested and extended the Kingdom of God to that extent.

The picture painted by the Hebrew prophets of God's reign on earth is one of abundance: the desert will blossom like a garden, and no mouth will lack for food. Isaiah says, ". . . they shall plant vineyards and eat their fruit" (65:21, RSV). The picture painted by the prophets is literally that of the Garden of Eden come back to life again. And, what is more, it is to happen *on the earth*, not at some future time in some other plane of life. This is not to say that it will not happen at some future time or on some other plane of life, but it means that it is not restricted to some distant future and far-off heaven.

In the vision of the Apocalypse, the Revelation of John, the writer talks about a new heaven and a new earth. Most of us can readily see the need for a new earth, but why the reference to a new heaven? Apparently the reason we need a new heaven and a new earth is that they are divided, separated from each other, and the heart demands that they merge with each other into a new creation. ". . . the tabernacle [the Holy of Holies, where God is] is with men . . . ," says John (Revelation 21:3). This is no different from the picture in the Old Testament. This demand, this dream, is man's nature and was placed within him at the very beginning of creation. It is a demand that must be fulfilled, or else man will continue to search and strive and demand until it is fulfilled.

Heaven means abundance and expansion; or at least abundance is one of the evidences of it. No one can imagine hunger and poverty in heaven; and the fact that mankind demand abundance, by their very nature, is proof and evidence that man was made for heaven and that the Kingdom of Heaven is already within him.

The Kingdom of Heaven within is evidenced by man's desire for life and not for death. He wants to live. He wants to live a full and long life. He does not accept death even when it comes. In primitive African cultures they cut a hole in the roof of the hut when a person was about to die, to enable the spirit to leave. They ate the flesh of animals and people, not always out of hunger and the desire for food, but to partake of their natures and spirits. Even in a primitive civilization we find man not really accepting death. The body might decay and rot, but they knew that the life was more than the body. Human nature, in the way it is created, is made for life and not for death.

Man was made for happiness, not for tears and sadness. Some of the most comforting verses in the Bible are concerned with a very important subject. In Revelation 21 it says, ". . . he [God] will wipe away every tear from their eyes, and death shall be no more, neither shall there be mourning nor crying nor pain any more, for the former things have passed away" (v. 4, RSV).

Many other traits of human nature might be cited, but surely the foregoing is enough. What it all means is that the instinctive nature of man, the way he was created, is in harmony with what we think of when we think of the nature of God. It may not be manifesting itself as it ought to, it may not be complete and perfect in expression, but the basic fact of man's nature is there and it reflects everything we think of when we think of God. Man was made for God and His Kingdom; his interior nature demands it. In this way the Kingdom of God "is within" us.

The Kingdom of God is *in the midst of you.* Scripture says that "The Lord thy God in the midst of thee is mighty . . ." (Zephaniah 3:17). Again it says that our bodies are the temple of

God. There is no cell or atom, there is no thought of our minds, and there is not a motivation or drive within us that is not God-created. We may not always express them as God intended—and in this way we thwart the intention of God—but God-created they are, unless we wish to make some sort of an argument for two gods. There is but One.

There is not a thing we can lay our eyes upon that is not God-created and in which all the possibilities of perfection reside. So the phrase, "in the midst of thee," must not be limited to the territory of our bodies, but must include the entire universe, things visible and invisible. In a way it is like saying that "we live, and move, and have our being . . ." *in* God (Acts 17:28).

When we say, "Thy kingdom come," we are saying, "Reveal and express Thy nature, Thy personality, Thy character, Thy name." We are asking God to strip life of everything that prevents the full expression of justice, peace, joy, love, abundance, patience, trust, faith, health, balance, wisdom, and anything else we associate with perfection. We are saying, "Come, break out in every area of living; manifest and extend the territory and the laws of living in such a manner that earth becomes heaven, and heaven becomes earth!"

And when we say, "Thy kingdom come," we are at the same time pledging ourselves to do everything possible to help out in this program of manifestation. Jesus told the disciples not only to preach the Good News of the Kingdom, but *to heal the sick.* In other words, they were to restore what had gone wrong to the original intent of God! We must restore to its rightful condition and heritage whatever has strayed from God's creative act where, when He looked upon it, it was "very good."

Jesus' actions were a walking illustration of this duty and pledge to restore to the heavenly pattern. The blind were made to see, the dead were raised, the hopeless got a new vision, those bound by tradition and wrong thinking were set free, and God was made real in a practical manner for everyone to enjoy.

A story is told about some missionaries who went to a remote part of India. As they talked to the people about Jesus of Nazareth and what He did, the people smiled and nodded their heads as if they knew all about Him. The missionaries were mystified by this reception and finally asked the people if they had heard the gospel before. They smiled and said they knew the one the missionaries were talking about. He had lived with them. After much questioning the missionaries finally got the story.

Another missionary had come to the people many years before, and had lived with them. He had been kind to them. He had healed their sick. He had given them new hope and made the God of the universe a Heavenly Father to them. Then he had died and left them. "Oh, yes," they said, "we know this one of whom you speak."

Jesus did the same thing in His time, only more perfectly. He not only talked about the Good News of the Kingdom of God; *He was the Good News,* and He extended the reign and rule and expression of the Kingdom of God wherever He was.

When one has this kind of knowing—the vision of God actually in manifestation in the soil, the rain, the moon; the relationships of man with man; the physical and mental activities of the human being; and the totality of life and beyond it—all he can do and yearn for and demand in exultation is "Thy kingdom come!"

It is also a moment-by-moment invitation to God to come in and reign and rule in one's own life, his body, mind, soul, and affairs. Jesus said that if we would ask, He and His Father would come *into* us and make their home with us. There is a condition to it. The condition is that they do *reign and rule.* It is on God's terms and not on our own.

When Dr. Frank Laubach had his life-changing experience in the Philippines he discovered the secret of letting God use his body. His life work seemed to have ended in failure. From high hopes and great ambitions he had suffered personal defeat after personal defeat until he did not know where to turn. It was in the depression of inner helplessness that he had gone up Signal Hill and sat down looking out over the ocean. There, in agony of soul, he asked God what was the matter with him, and the answer came back: "You do not love these people, Frank." He knew it was true, but he also knew that there was little he could do about it by himself.

"I know that, Lord," he said. "They are so dirty; their habits repulse me. I don't love them but I can't do anything about it."

Then came the secret that eventually turned a failure into a world-renowned figure and great ambassador for God.

"Let Me love them through you, Frank."

Here was the secret. There are things we cannot do on the human plane, as long as we rule ourselves. Only when God controls and reigns within us are some things possible.

So Frank Laubach began the "game with minutes," the game of making each moment a conscious communion with God. In this manner God did rule and control his mind, emotions, actions, facial expressions, everything. That very afternoon he met some priests of the Moros. Instead of avoiding them as he had previously done, he found himself going to meet them. He asked them if they would teach him the Koran. From that moment on he found he had broken through the barrier that had separated them. Friendships sprang up before long, and he found that his personal witness and the work he had always wanted to do moved ahead after being bogged down for so long.

This secret of *"God in you"* is further explained in the twelfth chapter of Romans: ". . . present your bodies as a living sacrifice, holy and acceptable to God, which is your spiritual worship" (v. 1, RSV). Present your bodies! for the free expression of justice, joy, peace, freedom—the Spirit which is God. In this way the Kingdom has come, beginning with you. Here also is the secret of the wisdom of Paul who says that it is God who works in us, both to will and to do His good pleasure. God in you, living, moving and manifesting—at His own pleasure or desire.

Jesus saw life that way, and He practiced it. When He said to Philip, "Have I been with you so long, and yet you do not know me, Philip? He who has seen me has seen the Father; how can you say, 'Show us the Father'? Do you not believe that I am in the Father and the Father in me? The words that I say to you I do not speak on my own authority; but the Father who dwells in me does his works. Believe me that I am in the Father and the Father in me; or else believe me for the sake of the works themselves" (John 14:9-11, RSV).

Jesus' body—His tongue, eyes, ears, hands, feet, mind, emotions —the entirety of him, was a *living* sacrifice presented to God the Father for God to work through and to manifest through and in—and it most assuredly did happen! Note the words that

Jesus used in this passage. God does not say the words that Jesus wants to say. God does not conform His purposes to Jesus' mouth and desire; it is the other way around. God does not do the works that Jesus wants to do; it is the other way around. *Jesus does the works that God wants to do:* "... the Father who dwells in me does *his* works."

When this happens, it is literally true that we shall ask whatever we will and it will be done, because we will be asking only what God "asks" in every situation, and the power of the universe will flow with us.

Charles Sheldon wrote a wonderful book called *In His Steps* in which the characters decided they would ask themselves before everything they did, "What would Jesus do?" I have heard some rather cynical people say, "How do you know what Jesus would do?" but there is no doubt that in many instances we would not do what we often do if we did ask ourselves this very question. Perhaps their opposition to the very idea is that they would rather not find out what Jesus would do, or might do. They want their own way too much. In Sheldon's book the lives of the people are completely transformed and charged with an attractiveness and power that is little short of miraculous. Glenn Clark wrote a sequel to the book and called it *What Would Jesus Do?* The characters are the grandchildren of the original characters, and of course the setting is in our more modern world with our different problems, but the results are the same. Transformation always takes place when our all-ness is brought under the dominion of God as expressed in that oneness revealed in Jesus Christ.

"Thy kingdom come"—manifest, reign, rule, express in all the earth, however long that might take.

"Thy kingdom come"—now, this moment, *in me.*

4

Thy Will Be Done

O F ALL the meanings and attitudes of the Lord's Prayer, this is the most important one. Without it, the rest of the prayer becomes but a high-flown ethic, a strong attraction worthy of striving after and emulating, and a technique whereby one might be able to bend the world to his own will and goal. With it, a man dies to himself, abdicates the throne of his own personality, and loses himself in Someone Else. We are all able to bring ourselves to heroic efforts of discipline and dedication, but the last barrier is giving up one's very life, and this is ultimately what it means to be truly able to say, "Thy will be done."

The words and actions of Jesus are an incarnate demonstration of the attitude of being lost in Someone Else. God was the most important fact in His life; every relationship of His life had meaning only as it related to this basic and prime fact. It was the cosmic hook upon which hung His whole outlook. He permitted nothing to stand in its way.

After Jesus had talked with the woman at the well, the disciples brought Him something to eat and He said, "My food is to do the will of him who sent me, and to accomplish his work" (John 4:34, RSV). The will, the purpose, the intention of God was food and drink to Him—His very life.

When His mother and brothers came to a house where He was holding a meeting, and the word was sent to Him that they were outside, Jesus said, "Who is my mother, and who are my brothers? . . . whoever does the will of my Father in heaven . . ." (Matthew 12:48, 50, RSV). His family had undoubtedly come to Him out of concern, however mistaken it was—or perhaps it was not mistaken from the human point of view. To gather a crowd about oneself, to be popular, to have the capacity of arousing people was not without danger. The Jewish rulers and the Roman conquerors did not take lightly such capacity for power in anyone else. If they thought He posed a threat to them, if they believed Him capable of stirring up trouble, He might simply disappear. Perhaps His family had reason to come looking for Him; but there comes a time in everyone's life when he has to do what will not be denied within himself, and evidently Jesus had come to that point. With the closeness that was typical of the average Jewish family of His time—and we might assume it was even more so in His particular family—it must have been difficult for Him to say what had to be said. In a way it meant cutting the bonds of family, however much it might be misunderstood and however much hurt it might cause. Apparently it had to be made public so that there would be no misunderstanding about it. We can be sure that eventually it was understood, as His mother continued to follow Him even to the cross where she was put in the charge of John the disciple. His brother James eventually became head of the church at Jerusalem, so there is no doubt that he came to an understanding also. Nothing is known about the rest of the family. It would seem reasonable that some of them did not understand. It would seem a bit incredible that they all would have been won over, but perhaps not.

There is little doubt that the greatest test anyone has to face is with his friends, not with his enemies. To withstand enemies may not always be easy, but there is little temptation about the issues involved. With friends it is a different matter. They have the key to our heart, to our love, and to our highest desires. We do not want to hurt them, even when it is necessary, and in many instances we fail at this very point. We give in, thinking that we are kind, when in reality we are confirming them in something that is not right. Jesus had to face up to the same temptations, and because He had totally surrendered Himself to the will of God He did not fail either Himself or His friends.

There is a ruthlessness here, an unbending and an uncompromising quality that might be mistaken for hardness and insensitivity. The common idea of Jesus "meek and mild" must be balanced with a dedication that is ruthlessly uncompromising.

Such an abandonment does not mean that the person will not almost revolt against it at times. In the Garden of Gethsemane, Jesus apparently needed the companionship of the disciples; at least He wanted them there while He prayed. All the humanness in Jesus wanted to feel the closeness of friends, the nearness of human flesh. But in the battles that are fought deep within the human citadel, in that secret place where no other man may intrude or is able to, man is alone with God, and God alone. Things of the world beckon and entice with all reasonableness on one hand, and often the deep interior knowing of God stands opposed to them. No one else makes a decision for another man in this territory of the soul. Each man makes his own. Our friends may be near us in person, but they cannot do it for us. They are always asleep.

In that desperately lonely test, Jesus made the decision, "Father, . . . not my will, but thine, be done" (Luke 22:42). The die was cast for the last time; from then on there was not even a remote possibility of compromise.

The account in the Gospel of Matthew shows that a titanic battle was fought in the Garden of Gethsemane. The first time when Jesus went apart to pray, it says, "And going a little farther he fell on his face and prayed, 'My Father, if it be possible, let this cup pass from me; nevertheless, not as I will, but as thou wilt'" (Matthew 26:39, RSV). He then arose and went back to the disciples to find them asleep, and He wakened them. What was He looking for? Help? Of some sort, if only the help of finding His friends waiting with Him; but He did not find even that. "Again, for the second time, he went away and prayed, 'My Father, if this cannot pass unless I drink it, thy will be done'" (v. 42, RSV). Once more He returned to His disciples, perhaps reaching out a hand for understanding, but again they were asleep. "So, leaving them again, he went away and prayed for the third time, saying the same words" (v. 44, RSV).

Who can possibly appreciate all that is contained in these few words? It can be assumed that there were more words spoken than are reported, but those that are reported reveal the basic issue. The issue was: His will or God's will.

Most people are afraid of the will of God. They believe it is opposed to their own deepest desires and goals. They are not sure that they want God to be interfering in their affairs.

I led a retreat for the men of a church. The theme was "Prayer." After one of my talks they broke up into little discussion groups to consider what had been said. As I visited each little group there was one concern that overshadowed everything else, and it was this matter of the will of God. The men were honest, and surely this is the starting point of all fruitful relationships with God, or with oneself.

One man said, "I am planning to take a trip to Europe this summer and I do not want God telling me that I can't go."

Another said, "I'm not sure that I want God poking around in my business. After all a man has to meet competition."

A young man in the advertising business put it this way: "I'm happy in the business I am in, and I have no desire to become a minister."

These remarks were indicative of the feelings of most of the other men. There were few who had little or no reservations, and some of them were retired men whose personal ambitions had waned.

The general attitude was that God's will in some way thwarted man's will. They were uncomfortable about their ideas and attitudes, but they were honest. No doubt they continued to think about it after the retreat was ended.

Until a man arrives at a conception of the will of God that is satisfying, prayer-power is bound to suffer and a man's life is weakened in the tension of indecision. The Creator is not "interfering" in the world out of vengeance and the desire to hurt. "God so *loved* the world, that he gave his only begotten Son, that whosoever believeth in him should not perish, but have everlasting life" (John 3:16). These are truly beautiful words, and yet how often they are spoken in tones that imply an angry God offering man a last chance—*or else!* The concern of God in this life is a *loving concern.* This is important and it is basic to all other considerations in the matter of the will of God. If we truly believe that God *is* love, then all His concerns must of necessity be loving concerns. A loving concern is one that benefits; it is one that puts the interest of the loved one foremost.

Love of this sort is a giving love; it is not a taking love. It is not a love that deprives anything essential or necessary to well-being or happiness. When a person is in love with a piece of work he gives it more time and energy than any amount of money could purchase. The one in love is not even aware of himself. His thought and concern are lost in the one being loved. He has lost himself in something else.

In a way it is the same with God. God is lost in humanity and all creation. He is working for it, for its perfect fulfillment, and for the 'perfect release of all its hidden potentialities. Jesus said, "... it is your Father's good pleasure to give you the kingdom" (Luke 12:32). Again, "If you then, who are evil, know how to give good gifts ... how much more will the heavenly Father ... to those who ask him?" (Luke 11:13, RSV). And what is a gift? If it is anything at all it is more than bare necessity. A gift is something beyond and above the mere fulfillment of duty. It is an expression of an abundance, perhaps something that is not necessary in the sense that necessity is the minimal need.

God enjoys, according to the mind of Jesus, doing good and giving pleasure toward the completion and fulfillment of our instinctive and intuitive dreams and wants. An old man once told me that God's ambition for me far surpassed any wild or impossible dream I had for myself. Surely life bears this out.

George Müller had a goal and a dream of being a minister in Germany. In the Germany of his day, the ministry was akin to a good civil service job. When he finally gave himself over to the will of God he never did achieve the security that he dreamed about as a minister of the state church. God had a bigger dream for him. He determined to look to God, and to God only, for all his sustenance. It is said that by the time he died, millions of dollars had passed through his hands, many hundreds of missionaries had been sent to all parts of the world, Christian literature was made available in quantities that are staggering, and orphanages had been built that housed and fed and educated numberless children. The influence of Müller still continues today to change men and set them to desiring a complete life with God. Certainly God's dream for Müller far exceeded the fondest dreams that Müller had for himself.

Dr. Frank Laubach had a dream for himself. Well-educated, his ambition was to be the president of a new seminary in the Philippine Islands. God had a better dream for him, and it began to come true when Frank Laubach gave up his own dreams and abandoned himself to God's will. Governments all over the world have called upon him for help to eradicate illiteracy. He has taught more people to read than any other person in the whole history of the world. God's dream was so much better.

These stories are common in history. God is not miserly; He is extravagant. He is extravagant in nature, and He is extravagant with men and women who give themselves over to His will. The amazing thing is that all these people say that in giving themselves over to His will they found what they had been looking for all along, *only more so!*

In the story of the feeding of the multitude, Jesus (as the revelation of God's will) did not merely provide a minimal amount. After the people had eaten, there was an abundance left over that was more than the amount they started with. God is extravagant!

This conception of the love of God, which is inseparable from His will, is not dependent upon our goodness or upon our badness. Reality is not compromised by our acceptance or rejection of it. Our acceptance or rejection has effects *upon us*, but not upon reality. If God is Love, our acceptance or rejection of that Love has little or nothing to do with the reality of it. The Scripture says this, or alludes to it, when it says, ". . . while we were yet sinners, Christ died for us" (Romans 5:8). He did not wait until we were worthy of it, or until we had mended our ways. God, of necessity, is simply true to His own nature, and that kind of a nature has got to manifest in a manner that is in harmony with itself. It too has to be loving, perfect, good, and abundant.

In spite of the fact that man may shy away from giving himself over to the will of God, there is a tendency within him that demands it. Louise Eggleston, a Methodist laywoman and conference speaker, has a way of illustrating this to people. At least she was the first person I have ever seen do it. I was once with her at a conference in Texas when she was speaking on the subject of prayer. Part of the way through her talk she stopped and said something like this:

"Suppose there were only one prayer in your entire life that would be answered? Suppose you could only ask God for one thing and get it? What would that request be? Remember, you can never go back and ask for anything else. You can only pray once, and get what you prayed for, and that is it. What will you ask for?"

She then had the group divide into smaller groups and go to different parts of the room to discuss it for five or ten minutes. When they came back into the large group she had them report on their decisions.

Without exception they all wanted the same thing—*the will of God for their lives*. Some of the words the people used were slightly different, but only slightly. It was amazing to note not only the complete accord of their ideas, but even the similarity of their words.

People of any degree of maturity realize that they do not know what is best for them. We have all had the experience of praying for something with the best and most sincere intentions in the world, only to find out that we were mistaken. I am convinced that if we could be sure of getting what we asked for in prayer, *all the time*, the time would soon come when we would be afraid to pray at all! Thank God that answered prayer also includes God's refusal to grant what we ask when it is wrong—either through our ignorance or intention.

Perhaps the most wonderful prayer-promise in the whole Bible is: "Likewise the Spirit helps us in our weakness; for we do not know how to pray as we ought, but the Spirit himself intercedes for us with sighs too deep for words. And he who searches the hearts of men knows what is the mind of the Spirit, because the Spirit intercedes for the saints according to the will of God" (Romans 8:26-27, RSV).

In other words, the Spirit helps us in our prayer-life by taking our prayers of finite limitation and saying something like this: "Heavenly Father, this man says that he wants this to happen, but what he is really striving after is *this*. . . . So, Father, answer the intention of the heart and not the words of his mouth."

Rufus Moseley, a modern saint if ever there was one, used to say that we must always pray and then say, or unspokenly desire, "Lord, this is the best I can think of in the situation, but if You have something better in mind, then cancel my prayer and give us Yours!"

This kind of prayer is vastly different from the resigned attitude of "if it be Thy will." To be more accurate, it is "According to Thy will." Man has doubted that his personal fulfillment is the will of God. He has wanted and searched for happiness, but he has not quite believed that God placed this striving within his breast. There was no such doubt in the mind of Jesus. He said, ". . . that my joy may be in you, and that *your joy* might be full" (John 15:11, RSV). Someone once asked Rufus Moseley if Jesus ever laughed, and he answered, "I don't know—but He sure fixed me up so I could."

To assent to the purposes and will of God, His plan, and the program as revealed within the human heart, is to come into perfect communion with life, to open the gates of possibilities within one's self, and to come into alignment with the laws of the universe.

A friend of mine had been troubled for some time with varicose veins in his legs. He was a rather large man, and whether his size had anything to do with the onset of the trouble, I do not know; but I do know that he was often in such pain that he was unable to stand on his feet. He had had a number of treatments and operations for the condition, but it seemed that nothing was of much help. As time went on he became quite depressed and discouraged.

After the last operation he was sent home. His wife and his mother agreed never to leave him alone as it was all but impossible for him to bear his weight. One night, quite by accident, they both had made arrangements to go out. When they realized that he would then be left alone, both of them wanted to cancel their engagements. However, he insisted that the women go and leave him alone; there was no need for them to stay home, he told them. He would prefer to be left alone as he had become uncomfortable about restricting their activities. So he had them place him in his favorite stuffed chair for the evening. If anything went wrong he could always crawl on his hands and knees. He assured them they had nothing to worry about.

After they had gone, my friend began to think about his condition. It seemed to him that he was fit for nothing. His life, he thought, was a failure. Life had lost its meaning. At some time in his reverie he found himself repeating the Lord's Prayer.

"You know," he told me, "I always did hedge on that phrase, 'Thy will be done.' But this time, as I came to it, I really meant it. I had completely given up on myself. I didn't seem to have any will of any kind left at all, and this time I wanted with all my heart to have God's will be done in me."

As he continued with the prayer and approached the end of it, "For thine is the kingdom . . . ," it seemed to him that the whole room was glowing with a fluorescence—the chairs, the table, the curtains, *everything!* The noise of automobiles in the street and the shouting of children outside, which just a few moments before had grated on his nerves, now seemed melodious.

Without conscious effort he found that he had stood up and walked over to the window to look out on the street. Everything was beautiful and alive, glowing with some sort of light that came from the inside of each object his eyes fell upon. He turned around and looked at the chair he had left, and suddenly the thought struck him, "Maybe I'm dead." He touched his own body. It had solid substance. Then he realized that if he were dead his body would still be in the chair!

Suddenly he was in the grip of fear and panic. He knew that he had to get back to the chair, or he would fall. With a desperate leap he reached the chair and sat there trembling. "Right then," he related, "I knew that fear was sin. Fear suddenly separated me from God. *Fear is sin!"*

It took him several months to get back to the place where he could walk again, but he learned something that has never left him. In perfect alignment with the will of God, what we call "miracles" are commonplace.

The will of God for us is far greater than we can imagine. What is God's intention or dream for the earth and the inhabitants of the earth? If we go back to the beginning of the Bible we find the story of creation. God brings all creation out of Himself. There is the separation of the firmaments, there is the dividing of the world into the dry land and the seas. Then God creates all the creatures of the earth, and finally He creates man. As each element or part of creation is formed, it is made by the command, "Let . . .": "Let there be a firmament . . ." (Genesis 1:6, RSV); "Let the waters under the heavens . . ." (v. 9); "Let the earth put forth vegetation . . ." (v. 11); "Let there be lights . . ." (v. 14); "Let the waters bring forth . . ." (v. 20); "Let the earth bring forth living creatures . . ." (v. 24); "Let us make man . . ." (v. 26).

The word "let" gives the impression that something is already there waiting to be permitted to happen. Certainly God the Spirit was there, and we must assume He was the only Reality before manifested creation. To let something happen must have meant to remove any barriers that would prevent it. Perhaps, in our terms, it was merely an illustration of what we might call "thinking." When we decide to do something, or think about doing something, in order for it to happen we "let" or permit something in our wills to remove any barrier to the happening. *We let it happen.*

That might be the meaning of the "letting" of creation. God desired creation and then "let" or permitted it to manifest. It was an indication of His will; He willed it; He wanted it. It was not something that forced itself into being from some outside source. Creation is the desire, or the good pleasure, of God.

As God is complete and perfect goodness in every manner we can imagine, the end result of creation follows quite logically: "And God saw everything that he had made, and behold, it was very good" (v. 31). As creation was the outer manifestation of God's nature, how could it help but be anything else but "very good?" It would have to be that way.

What came about from these acts of creation is what is known as "The Garden of Eden." In this story of the manifested character of God, the whole earth is in perfect harmony, peace, and abundance. It is a projection, a picture of the mind or nature of the Creator. "So God created man in his own image, in the image of God he created him; male and female he created them. And God blessed them, and God said to them, 'Be fruitful and multiply, and fill the earth and subdue it; and have dominion over . . .'" (vv. 27-28).

There is another story of creation in the second chapter of Genesis: ". . . then the Lord God formed man of dust from the ground, and breathed into his nostrils the breath of life; and man became a living being" (v. 7).

There is not necessarily any conflict between these two stories. One reveals the mind of God and the fact that all creation came forth by the function of His will. It does not describe the manner in which it took place. There is no reason why the creative technique could not be symbolized by the second story. Both accounts are but two parts of one complete story—the story of creation.

The two stories of creation are reflected in the nature of every human being. Part of man is incapable of being limited by his earthly nature and body. Man is of the earth, earthy; but he is not confined to the earth. His mind and spirit fly not only beyond the confines of his own body, but they penetrate the surface of manifested creation and explore the invisible. He is as much at home considering such subjects as infinity, love, faith, God, purpose, and meaning as he is concerned with sticks and stones, flesh and blood, and tools and soil. The result of creation within his own nature reflects the Biblical stories of creation that merge the spirit with flesh, mind with matter, and God with man.

We have already talked about the "name" as meaning the nature or the essence of intrinsic being. There is an interesting sidelight on this in the story of creation, and it also sheds light on the will of God: "So out of the ground the Lord God formed every beast of the field and every bird of the air, and brought them to the man to see what he would call them; and whatever the man called every living creature, that was its name. The man gave names to all cattle, and to the birds of the air, and to every beast of the field . . ." (Genesis 2:19-20, RSV).

In the beginning, the creatures of the earth "knew" each other. They were not ruled by fear, nor did they prey upon each other. Apparently they lived in harmony, and this harmony included man.

The Hebrew prophets describe the reign and rule of God on the earth (referring to some future time) as a period when the animal kingdom and man will live in peace and harmony; the lion will lie down with the lamb, the child will put its hand into a snake's den without hurt, and the bear will eat straw like an ox. Today we still believe it is possible, under the right conditions, for man and wild animals to live in peace and harmony. One of the best-sellers in recent years was the story of a man and his wife who reared a lioness from babyhood, and how the lioness even brought her cubs for them to see after she was full-grown. In spite of many evidences to the contrary, we still dream of such a condition being common rather than the exception. Could this dream be but a forgotten memory of a beginning that actually was that way?

Surely this dream of perfection is evidence of a deep intrinsic faith. ". . . faith is the *substance* of things hoped for, the *evidence* of things not seen" (Hebrews 11:1). One fine bit of logic would be to ask ourselves if there is anything that man is capable of thinking about that is not capable of taking place. How can we think of something that is "not"? Human history is the story of man's dreams always leaping ahead of his achievements and present possibilities; and it is also the story of these dreams, these fantastic imagings, eventually taking place. The Garden of Eden, a perfect beginning in which God and man and all creation are in perfect harmony and abundance, is a dream (or lingering memory?) that is common to mankind.

One theme runs through the stories and parables of Jesus. The earth really belongs to God, but wicked and rebellious servants have usurped power and turned traitor. All His stories end with the master, or the king, returning to claim his territory and to punish those who have rebelled. Here is some insight into the mind of Jesus and the "will of God" as He saw it. There is the parable of the master who left his vineyard in the keeping of his servants. They enjoyed the privilege and the power and decided to keep it for themselves. The master sent other servants to collect what was due him, and the rebellious servants beat them and sent them away. Finally the master said that he would send his own son, so that they would surely recognize and obey him. But they took the son and killed him, thinking that if they got rid of the heir, the vineyard would surely be theirs. Jesus said that the master would then come and destroy the wicked servants.

To Jesus, the will of God was at once a vision of perfection upon the earth, and also a commission to expend Himself in the task of restoring earth to the original intention of God. This commission was not a retreat from the starkness of reality. He did not shut His eyes to the injustices about Him; He was more aware of them than if He had never known the will of God. He did not retreat within Himself to escape the harshness of social conditions; He threw Himself into the melee of human society to improve it and to make it more nearly reflect the will of God as He saw it. His relationship with God did not drug His senses or cushion the blows of fate; rather it made Him more sensitive to and aware of them.

When the rich young ruler came to Jesus, He identified his condition (or sickness) with the incisive insight of a great psychiatrist of the soul. He showed him the trouble, and He also pointed the way to freedom and health. When the young man was unable (or at that moment incapable) to do what he was told, it is said that "Jesus looking upon him loved him . . ." (Mark 10:21, RSV). Jesus was too lost in God to feel the rejection as a personal affront.

We often treat our children like that. We know that someday they will have to do many things that they are incapable of doing right now. Depending upon their ages, they will have to go to school, write papers, speak before people, drive an automobile, get married, have children, and do many other things. We do not condemn them for not doing what they will eventually have to do before they are of an age to do them.

There are also people who reach an age where they ought to be able to do certain things, but they are not capable. There has been some lack in their training, some mental or emotional failure to grow up and adjust to the demands of life (or perhaps some physical difficulty accounts for their inability); but anyone who knows them and is familiar with their conditions cannot condemn them. Instead, the more we understand and know about them, the more love and compassion we have for them.

A good friend of mine once said, "If an apple is green and sour, don't curse it. Just wait awhile." How wise! If we would treat people with the same wisdom and consideration, the perfection of God would be much more manifest than it is. The wisdom and understanding of Jesus in His treatment of the rich young ruler—the fact that He looked on him and loved him even though the young man did not follow Him—brought the will and impression of God to bear upon him. Who is to tell what happened to the rich young ruler in later years because Jesus looked at him and *loved him?*

So, when Jesus revealed His interior attitudes by saying, "Thy will be done . . . ," He was asking for the right individual and social relationships to be manifested now, and He was envisioning and affirming the intention of God for the future as well.

For one thing, He was asking for a new spirit to invade and control the consciousness of man. Someone has said that it would do little good if the riches of the world were evenly distributed among the peoples of the earth; within a few hours men would be robbing each other, and others would find cunning ways to part the unsuspecting from their new-found wealth.

If, in a twinkling of an eye, the Garden of Eden were once more manifested on earth, how long would it remain so if man were driven by the same spirit that he now has, attracted by the same ambitions that he now has, ruled by the same passions that rule him now? In a short time the Garden of Eden would cease to exist and a kind of a semi-hell would take its place. The possibilities for the Garden of Eden would still be there, but the spirit or will to "let it be" would be lacking. Good things used wrongly result in pain and frustration, and perfect relations are destroyed both inwardly and outwardly.

Scientists say that there are all the possibilities for heaven on earth right now. The building blocks are here, but they are being used wrongly, and they will continue to be used wrongly until we get a new spirit, a new will, a new intention, a new ambition, and a new center. This is the reason for, the all importance of *"Thy will be done. . . ."*

5

In Earth, as It Is in Heaven

THE four conceptions of the first part of the Lord's Prayer are conditioned by "on earth as it is in heaven." Mere improvement is not enough, nor is it the intention of God, according to the mind of Jesus. The goal is perfection—"On earth as in heaven." God, and life itself, is content with nothing short of it. In the mind of Jesus there was a war to be won, and it would never be won until earth was like heaven, and heaven was like earth.

What would be the results of this prayer, this framework of attitudes, if it came true? Earth, as we know it, and heaven, as we know it, would be things of the past. The thing that makes heaven heaven is the perfect and complete expression of the nature of God. As far as creation is concerned, it would be the perfect outpicturing of the nature of God through the medium of creation; not just a partial expression as we now have, not just the "seeing through a glass darkly," but the full and unrestrained expression of God in every atom of creation. This *is* heaven. So when Jesus prays, desires, wills, and envisions the first part of the Lord's Prayer, He is seeing the union of the invisible and the visible, the eternal and the temporal, the partial and the whole, the there and the here, the future and the present, the flesh and the spirit, the perfect and the imperfect—all in perfect harmony, accord, and oneness.

When Jesus said, "Be ye therefore perfect, even as your Father which is in heaven is perfect" (Matthew 5:48), He was not talking about an accomplished fact of expression, but rather about a complete dedication to the vision and the ideal, a total abandonment to the total will and nature of the Father, a completely un-inhibited giving of one's self over to a great commission.

He talks about the rain falling on the good and on the evil, and about the sun shining on the just and on the unjust. The point that He is making is that our actions and reactions ought to be predictable and uninhibitedly dependable. We ought to love not only those whom we normally love, but our love ought to include the unlovely too. We ought to do good not only to those we normally do good to; we ought to do good to those to whom we normally do not do good. This amounts to a complete reaction pattern that is not comprised by our natural likes and dislikes. Our emotions and attitudes must not be determined by the in-consistencies of others, or we ourselves become inconsistent, com-pletely unlike God, and reduced to a lower level of living.

It is not our job to sit in judgment on the possible effectiveness of our efforts. It is our job to "do what God would do" in a given situation and leave the results to God. We are to scatter the seeds of our efforts with the abandonment of the sower. Some may fall by the wayside, some may be wasted among the thorns, and some may fall among the rocks. That is not our concern. We are to do the job of sowing as if all our seeds were falling in good soil and multiplying themselves. This is perfect consistency of action and reaction. This is being perfect, "as your Father . . . in heaven is perfect." God's laws, the expression of His nature in nature, are not compromised by our acceptance or rejection. God *is* (the same yesterday and today and forever), and this unendingness of goodness and love will be triumphant.

This being perfect, "as your Father . . . in heaven is perfect," is therefore not an accomplished condition of existence. Heaven in manifestation upon the earth is not here yet; it is in a process of becoming through the totality of the action-reaction frame-work of our dedication to the nature of God. The perfect is al-ways and continuously being poured into the imperfect. God is constantly breaking through into human society, and into all nature, through the medium of human personalities that belong to Him. Because of them heaven is becoming more earthy; and the earth is becoming more heavenly. When the job is complete, earth will be swallowed up in heaven and heaven will be swallowed up in earth. Former dichotomies will cease to exist; all things will have become new. There will be a new heaven and a new earth—each lost in the other; old things will have passed away.

It is this lostness in each other that is the dream and demand of the entire first half of the Lord's Prayer. There is little consolation in the last half of the Lord's Prayer if it does not spring from the vision of the first half. The improvement of our earthly lot—which is what the second part of the Prayer is about—would then become but techniques for improving or making more endurable a meaningless and pointless existence.

"On earth as it is in heaven" means that Jesus will be satisfied with nothing short of the complete and perfect return of the earth to the picture we have of the Garden of Eden. If God's nature is recognized and loved and revered, if all creation is sensitive and responsive to Him and is the perfect outpicturing of His nature and personality, and if His intention and goal and will are perfectly demonstrated in creation, then we are in heaven. Heaven is then an accomplished fact; Creator and creation are one, lost in perfect relationship with each other, inseparable. This was the dream, the vision Jesus had for earth. This was the goal that drove Him on and brooked no opposition and made compromise impossible. Becoming an earthly king was little temptation to Him when this was the goal He had in mind. The most that earth had to offer Him—and that is summed up in the story of His temptations by Satan—could not come close to matching such perfection.

"On earth as it is in heaven" is the pearl of great price. Once a man sees it he will sell all that he has to buy it, to make it come true. Once the perfect has been seen—even if only for a split second—the imperfect can never really satisfy again. This interior vision, this total yearning, was the source of Jesus' actions and the headwaters of His motivations and drives. In this relationship to the nature of God, it follows that He had to be out of relationship with the way men were ruling the world and themselves. He was in perfect adjustment to God; therefore He was out of adjustment to everything less than God.

"On earth as it is in heaven" was not a rejection of the world. This was His Father's world, whether or not the world knew it. It was His Father's world, and the purpose of His life, His coming, His death, and His resurrection was to bring the two back into a right relationship. By His behavior, as well as by His words, He has caused men to raise their sights to heights they never contemplated before; He made them dream of possibilities of living that only God could satisfy. He did not cut the cloth of His life to conform to what was reasonable or expedient in the world. His pattern was the complete majesty of God, visible in all creation, invisible in all transcendency. His job was not to conform, but to transform—Himself first, and then the whole earth.

"On earth as it is in heaven" was the core-thought and deepest desire of Jesus, the wellspring of all His words and actions, the divine obsession driving all creation to oneness with God.

6

Give Us This Day Our Daily Bread

N I Chronicles 29:14 we read that "all things come of thee [Lord], and of thine own have we given thee." *All* things! Not just religious things.

When Jesus said, "Give us this day our daily bread," it was at once an acknowledgment of the Source and a readying of His expectancies to receive from that Source. In perfect harmony with the Father, He was in perfect harmony with the laws of supply and demand as well as all other laws. It is an interior relationship, and conscious affirmation, that places a person naturally and spontaneously in the right place at the right time for the flow of abundance that God has already built into the structure of living. The interior relationship is all-important.

A young married man decided that he had to go back to college and finish his education. The only job he could get that would enable him to go to school and work at the same time was selling brushes from door to door. He told me, "As long as my wife and I relied utterly upon God, there did not seem to be too much to selling enough to meet our needs, with some left over. Everything seemed to go quite smoothly."

Then with a wry smile he continued, "But, you know people— all of us. It isn't long before we begin to think that *we* are doing it. We begin to think that we are experts at selling, and we begin to take all the credit for our success. Prayer times become perfunctory. We are merely tipping our hats to God, and not too sincerely at that.

"Every time this happened to me, my selling went to pot. As far as I could tell, I was acting the same way and I was saying the same things. But I just wasn't selling. For a while we would think that perhaps the cause of the failure was that it was some special time of the month—such as around the tenth, when people had to pay their bills. It soon became apparent that the time of the month, or anything else, had nothing to do with it.

"When our finances got to the point where we were nearly broke, we always got on our knees—literally on our knees—and prayed, and each time we were made to know exactly what was wrong. We had ceased depending upon God and had slipped over into depending upon ourselves.

"Of course we got back on the beam right away. Again, each morning, we got down on our knees, for we knew what our Source was—God! Once more I would go out, and as far as I can tell I did what I had always done. I rang doorbells and said the same things to people that I had always said. But there was a difference. *I made sales!*"

"Give us this day our daily bread" is a statement of trust. It is asking for the bread of the day, and not a hoard for the future. A lady who lived this way was told by someone, "That sure is an easy way to live!" Her reply was, "If you think it is, try it sometime!" Our difficulties stem from lack of trust—lack of trust in God. If we really had a close walk with God, if He were truly real to us, we would have little concern for the future. We would not know more of the future than we do right now, but we would know the One who does know the future; and because we know Him and His goodness we would know that the future is secure and in beneficent hands. We would then give ourselves more fully to the demands and opportunities of the present moment.

A good friend of mine was very concerned about the future for her son. When the weight of worry and fear became so heavy that she could not stand it any longer, the words of an old hymn, a favorite of her father, came to her mind:

So long thy hand has led me, Still it shall lead me on.

Trust and assurance returned to her almost immediately.

"Give us *this* day our *daily* bread." When Moses was leading the children of Israel through the wilderness toward Canaan, there came the time when it looked as if the people would die of starvation. Then we read the story of the manna. When the people asked what it was—that strange substance lying on the early-morning ground—"a fine, flake-like thing, fine as hoarfrost . . ." (Exodus 16:14, RSV), Moses told them:

"It is the bread which the Lord has given you to eat. . . . Gather of it, every man of you, as much as he can eat; you shall take an omer apiece, according to the number of persons whom each of you has in his tent." And the people of Israel did so; they gathered, some more, some less. But when they measured it with an omer, he that gathered much had nothing over, and he that gathered little had no lack; each gathered according to what he could eat. And Moses said to them, "Let no man leave any of it till the morning." But they did not listen to Moses; some left part of it till the morning, and it bred worms and became foul; and Moses was angry with them. Morning by morning they gathered it, each as much as he could eat; but when the sun grew hot, it melted.

Just enough for one day, and no more. Only enough for the day, gathered morning by morning. It was natural for some of them to want to put away a little for the next day, but God had arranged it in such a way that it could not be done—the bread spoiled and bred worms. I am sure they made some very good arguments about the wisdom of putting some of it away, but in the emergency situation God did not let them upset what He knew was necessary to their survival. All too often we make many high-sounding and wise arguments to cover up what really amounts to our lack of faith.

Many people shake their heads when one begins to talk about trust and supply only for the day. "Aren't we supposed to plan for the future?" they ask. Within reason, I am sure that we are, but what is the best way to prepare for the future? The best way is to learn how to live life fully in the present moment. If we do a good job of living in the now, the tomorrows will automatically take care of themselves.

The head of a large corporation once told me that they got the heads of their departments from the men who were already in the organization. "When a promotion is to be made we naturally look over the many men who might fill the job. You know, there is seldom much doubt in our minds about who ought to have the job. The man who has proven himself by dependability, study, and experience over the years almost always floats to the surface.

If he has done good work in each job he has held in the corporation, he is simply the one who stands out."

"Give us this day our daily bread" is not an invitation to laziness. In the case of Moses and the children of Israel and their experience with the manna, God did not literally feed them; He did not put the strange food into their mouths. I am sure it would have been possible for God to fill their mouths with the manna in some miraculous manner, but He did not do it that way. The manna was on the ground and *they had to do the gathering.* Scripture says that the manna was like flakes; in other words, it was very small, and it must have taken a lot of gathering to get the required amount. The people had to go out and work. Depending upon God day by day means that we must work and seek out whatever it is we are after. God has built society and the world of society in such a manner that He works and manifests through the normal avenues of the human mind and social and natural relationships.

Sometimes we see little possibility of God working in the normal complexities of society, but that is the common manner in which He does work. If a person wants a job, it is his duty and responsibility to explore employment agencies and the personnel offices of businesses where he would like to work. There is no agency or office in which God does not have entree. Those in charge of an employment office may not be thinking of God or the laws of life, but it is not necessary that they do so. However, it is necessary for the man of God who is seeking a job to be aware that God is working for him and through him. *In right relationship with God, who is Spirit in and through all of life, man comes into right relationship with creation, and creation includes an employment agency just as much as anything else.*

One man told me that when he goes into an office, whether looking for a job or for any other reason, he has gotten into the habit of thinking within himself, "The Christ in me salutes the Christ in you." He does not do it only in times of want and need; it has become a habit that permeates all his relationships. It has changed his world from a lonely strangeness to a friendly ease. The world, for him, has become "my Father's world," and he is but seeking out what God has already prepared for him. He knows that God is there, that God has already been there before him, wherever he is; and so he finds himself expressing more fully and confidently the potentialities within himself which God placed there.

This claiming of God's ever-present involvement in one's affairs is the secret of David, the shepherd boy who became a great king. In I Chronicles 14 he asks God if he should do battle with the Philistines. He is told to go ahead and that God will give them into his hand. After the defeat of the Philistines, David says, "God has broken through my enemies *by my hand*, like a bursting flood" (v. 11, RSV). There was no doubt about the One to whom David gave credit; God was responsible for David's victory, and he knew it. But God did not do it alone, and this is important. God did it *through the obedient hand of David*. Without the hand of David, God would not have had the opportunity to manifest His power and wisdom.

One wonders how many more great victories have never been won because a man was unwilling to commit himself. God is always willing to commit Himself! The power and the wisdom of God is always there, waiting to burst out like a flood, whenever the opportunity is presented. It does not have to be a military battle; it can be a battle with inner fear and inferiority, or it can be a battle of seeking a job.

A friend of mine travels over many states in his job as a salesman. The story of his career illustrates the difference it makes when one becomes God's man. He had attempted this same job three times before, and each time he had failed at it. The time came when life had worn him down to the point where he gave his life over into the hands of God.

"There wasn't much to give," he told me. "Only failure and heartsickness. But I did it, anyway. God was my only hope."

He determined that the first hour of each day would be spent in prayer and reading the Bible and his prayer book. No matter where he was, he kept the tryst. As most of his nights were spent in motel rooms, many a motel room became a little altar between this man and his God. The result is that he is now successful in his work, and he has proved that God does provide his daily bread.

Something else happened. Little by little many of his customers began to confide in him about their problems, and he found himself pointing these people to the same Source that he had found. Counseling with others was a job that he had never thought of doing; it was an overflow, an evidence that the invisible God was working in and through him.

"You know," he told me, "I get a strange and thrilling feeling, something like awe, when I drive over these roads in my work. These roads used to be roads of frustration and discouragement. I was so alone and frightened. Everything was going wrong with me. I was a failure and ashamed of it, but I didn't know what to do about it. Now I drive along these same roads and they are friendly roads. It is the same with many of the people I call upon. I used to call upon them with no effect at all. Now I call on them and I make sales and find them my friends. I am so often in a state of wonder, just like a little kid. I know God is the only answer."

The story of Jesus and the miraculous draught of fish (Luke 5:1-11) is a perfect example of what this man was talking about. Simon and Andrew and James and John had fished all night and had caught nothing. As they were washing their nets, Jesus came by and asked if He could talk from their boat to the crowd that followed Him. He was given permission. Would He have had that chance if Peter had caught fish that night? I doubt it. Peter and his partners would have been so busy working over their fish that they would probably have had little time for an itinerant preacher. Who knows how many nights they had been unsuccessful in their search for fish? They could have been quite desperate in a financial way. The East Indians have a saying, "When the student is ready, the master appears." There is a lot of truth in it. When we are ready and willing, God always appears in some form. At any rate, Peter permitted Jesus to enter his boat to do His work.

When Jesus finished talking with the people, He turned to Simon and said, "Put out into the deep . . . for a catch" (v. 4, RSV). They protested that they had been out all night and had caught nothing. Then Peter said something that is all-important: "But at your command, we will do it." Here again is the secret of obedience: the *willingness* to obey is all-important. If we are going to wait continually until "we can see it," then there will be a lot of life we will never taste, and a lot of discoveries we will never make.

The next important thing to notice about this story is that Jesus got into the boat with them. He did not stand on the shore and tell them to go off by themselves; He went with them, and that is illustrative of our life with God. God is not a distant and separated Being. He is continually and constantly within us, without us, all about us, and there is no place we can go where God is not. Even the Psalmist says, ". . . if I make my bed in hell, behold, thou art there" (139:8). It does not matter what one's affairs are; God is there already, He does not have to be called from some distant abode.

And remember, Jesus told the fishermen to put out into the deep *for a catch*. When it comes to positive thinking, this is it! He did not tell them to put out and go fishing, but to put out *for a catch*. It would not be wasted effort. It would result in fish.

So they put out, taking Jesus along with them, and they enclosed a school of fish so great that they had to call upon their partners for help. The event filled Peter with such awe and fear that he fell on his knees and said to Jesus, "Depart from me, for I am a sinful man . . ." (Luke 5:8, RSV). Peter knew that something so unusual had happened that the only explanation for it had to be God. He realized that Jesus was in league with God, and when one realizes he is truly in the company of a Man of God, or a God-Man, by comparison he realizes the poverty of his own nature. It is an awesome experience. Then Jesus told Peter not to be surprised, but that from now on he would catch men. The methods used in the catching of fish are also to be used in catching men: obedience and commitment to the Word and command of God.

There is another lesson to be learned from this story. *Peter and his partners were not taken out of their circumstances.* They were not shielded from the responsibilities of life. They were not plucked out of their environment and placed in a more desirable place. They had to find God where they were, doing the ordinary things they did every day. They had to go into the same waters, use the same nets and the same boat, and apply the same skills. Everything to the outer eye was exactly the same as it had always been. There was just one difference: they had taken Jesus into their boat and their business, and they were obedient to His command. That alone was what made the difference. And, that alone, is what always makes the difference!

Give us this day our daily bread! Don't expect to be fed by the ravens while you are making no effort. God seldom works in such a manner. Almost always He works through your mind, and your body, and your efforts. If they are dedicated to Him, He will "burst through your enemies like a flood" but it will almost always be accomplished "by your hand."

Trust God; know He is your Source; that it is His good pleasure and joy to provide; that the provision is already there; and that His indwelling Spirit is what puts you into the right place at the right time for abundance.

Alan Redpath tells a wonderful story of his life. He had started a fund which he called "God's Fund." It was money which people had given him to help others. During the days of World War II this fund was at the lowest point it had ever been. Alan Redpath was an air-raid warden, and one morning at dawn he was walking his area and thinking about "God's Fund." He was carrying on a mental conversation with God about it. Somewhere in the conversation he was asked why he thought the fund was so low and he gave all kinds of reasons for it: the war was on, people had their minds on other things, so and so, who was a good contributor to the fund, had died, and so on. Then the Word of God burst on his mind with forceful clarity: "So you have come to rely upon people instead of Me!"

Immediately Alan Redpath knew it was right; he was convinced by the wrongness of it. Right there, on the street, he got down on his knees and asked God to forgive him, and promised God that from then on he would never take the eyes of his expectancy off Him. Within a very short time there was more money in the fund than it had had for years. Money came from all over the British Isles and from people Redpath had never known before.

Give us this day our daily bread is above all the realization that God is the Source of all aspects of life, including the source of our incomes. When one looks at his paycheck, he ought to think that the money came from the Father through the intermediary of whatever firm it is he is working for. The firm does not have to be aware of it, but the recipient must never forget it if he is to enter into a freedom of life that is impossible any other way.

Give us this day our daily bread has another meaning that we must never forget; it is contained in the little word "us." It is not only daily bread for myself, but it is also daily bread for everyone else. Just recently a very successful businessman told me that when he prayed for himself he also prayed for his competitors; and he prayed the same kind of prayer for his competitors that he prayed for himself. Our daily bread must never come at the expense of anyone else. There is enough for all, and more than enough. To the extent that we would do harm to another —even the harm that would come from wishing them bad fortune—we do harm to ourselves. We cannot shut the door of flow and abundance to anyone else without shutting those same doors to ourselves. Abundance, one aspect of the personality of God, cannot be contained any more than God Himself can be contained.

I have seen people become anxious and worried over the success of someone else. They think that when other people are making money, it is money taken out of their own pockets. Soon they become small with envy and fear, and it is not long before they find the gates of God's everflowing abundance shut to themselves.

In I Corinthians 13 we read that love rejoices in the right. Love, which is God, rejoices in any full expression of itself, whether it be the abundance of peace or joy or faith or material things. If we are completely dedicated to the manifestation of God on earth (and obtaining our daily bread is one of those manifestations) then we should be happy over the good fortune of others. It is vitally necessary to rejoice in the success of our competitors. Their success is a demonstration that the laws of God's supply are working in and through that business. The same laws of God's supply are working in and through us when we are in proper relationship with our Father in heaven. If we are not capable of rejoicing over the success of another, then we have precious little right to expect it to flow in our own direction.

A man has a little grocery shop near my home. A large building was erected two doors from him and everyone wondered what it would be. When the news got out that it was to be a modern supermarket, everyone felt sorry for the man. They were sure that it meant the end of his business which had been there for many years. "It's too bad—but you can't stop progress," said someone expressing the attitude of most everybody.

It was not too bad. It was too good! The supermarket brought crowds of people to that corner who had never even thought of it before. Many people were embarrassed to pass by the grocery store window after they had been trading there for so long, but with a larger variety and lower prices at the supermarket it was inevitable that they would do so. However, there was always enough overflow to make up for those who passed by. In fact, his business was better than before the supermarket came.

For reasons which I do not know, the supermarket closed after some years. The little grocery shop is still there and, from all anyone can see, it will be there for as long as the owner wishes to remain in business. If that small grocery store owner had heaped abuse on his old customers, or failed to maintain a sunny disposition and friendly attitude during those years, he would not have gained the overflow and he would have lost his old friends, too. His spirit and attitude made the difference.

It is common knowledge among business people that whenever a large company makes a national mailing, everyone benefits from it. It is true that the company making the mailing makes the most profit from it, but there is always enough overflow from the publicity to benefit little shops all over the country. People look at what is advertised and then they often go to their own shops and ask for it. By cold economic fact we have to give thanks to God for the large company in competition with us. That company benefits us, too, whoever we are.

Rejoicing in the good fortune of others is an important secret of a full life. If we are going to limit our joy and contentment exclusively to our own efforts and affairs, then we are going to miss most of the joys of living. Life becomes superabundantly rich and worthwhile when we share in the joy of others. Entering into the joy of others makes life whole. We do it every day in literature, art, science, and business. The man who lives to himself is a poverty-stricken personality. When we find our rest *in God*, realizing that others are not threats to us at all, then we will naturally share in the satisfactions of others. We can never be complete without others—no more so in the spiritual realm than we can in the business realm. Jesus said, "I have come that your joy might be full. Enter into my joy."

Give us this day our daily bread also means that we must not hoard what we have. The flow must be constant and continual; it must not stop with us. By hoarding we stop the flow.

In the feeding of the five thousand, Jesus took the little bit that He had to work with and first of all blessed it. This is important. If one is not willing to bless, to thank God for the little he has, then there is little evidence that he will do better with more. Practically all businesses, or forms of income, begin small. It is the exceptional case when a full-blown source of income is placed at the disposal of anyone. What one now has, regardless of how large or how small, is a seed of possibility. With the right environment and climate, it can grow (and remember, seeds do not grow by addition; they grow by multiplication). To reject what one has is to restrict or kill the growth possibilities that are already there. It is lack of faith.

Too often we look at our "seed of possibility" with human eyes. We are like Andrew who brought to Jesus the little boy with the five loaves and two fish and said, ". . . but what are they among so many?" (John 6:9, RSV). Jesus showed us the secret of overcoming in such a situation. He took what there was, knowing that with God all things are possible, and that God is not limited by the limitations of our minds. He took the food in His hands, raised His eyes to heaven, and blessed it.

His eyes did not linger on the poverty of the situation. He looked to the source of all things—to heaven, the expression of God's fullness—and He gave the poverty of the situation to the abundance of God.

Rufus Moseley used to say that if a poor girl married a rich man her poorness would be swallowed up in his richness. When she lost herself in another who was rich, at that very moment her poverty ceased to exist; her husband's richness, flowing into every area of her poverty, would transform it. So it is with a man and his God. His littleness is swallowed up in God's bigness, and his poverty is swallowed up in God's richness. Paul says, "Now unto him that is able to do exceeding abundantly above all that we ask or think . . ." (Ephesians 3:20). This is a God without limitations, and the size of our offering is really of no importance. Even if our offering were large in our own sight, it would still be little in the eyes of God. If one truly knows this, he will take his eyes away from the poverty of whatever the situation is, but he will not reject the situation. He will look to the place of abundance (heaven) and permit that place to swallow up the poverty by flowing into it.

How is one to do it? Ought he to sit by and wait for a miracle? No, that is not what Jesus taught us in this story. He took what He had and began to break it up, and He gave it to His disciples, and the disciples gave it to the multitude. Use what you have! Because of its smallness, do not clutch it to yourself for fear of losing it. Put it to use. Work! And, in the working, in the flow and the ebb, in the give and in the take, it is surprising what a little will become. Only in action, in putting something to use, will anything grow. Even a muscle of the body will wither and become useless if it is not exercised. Life is the same way. Only as it is used will it produce and multiply. The flow in the Scriptural instance was from heaven, or from God, to Jesus, to the disciples, and finally to the multitude. What would have happened if one of the disciples had thought, "After all, I am one of the inner circle. I am as hungry as anyone else. I have a right to be fed first"? The flow would have stopped. There would have been no miracle.

A man who started a business in a small way exemplified the point of putting the seed to work. He began manufacturing a resin and oil for the floors of large auditoriums and buildings. Finally he was able to get some salesmen, who were carrying other products, to carry his, too. He told me, "In those years I got mighty discouraged, and wondered if I had not gotten into the wrong business. I worked long, hard hours to supply orders which the salesmen sold. I slept on a cot in the back of the shop. The salesmen were making a lot more money than I, but I kept at it, and the time came when there were so many orders that I had to hire extra help, and after some time I began to reap the benefits of keeping at it."

His business began as just a little seed. It was not much. It was rather pitiful in comparison to national companies supplying similar products. By using the "five loaves and two fish" which he had, and by distributing them, they multiplied themselves into a company of national prominence.

At a retreat in California one of the men was an alcoholic and had become a member of Alcoholics Anonymous. He had been looking for a job for over a year, and although he was experienced in the construction business, he did not seem to be able to find work. An awakening interest in God, through another man who was there, had resulted in his attendance at the retreat. Someone suggested that we pray for him. In that atmosphere of dedication and yieldedness to God and His will, the prayer was a complete throwing of ourselves on the Person of God. The whole group joined in the prayer, asking that the need and the satisfaction of the need might find each other. A day later I had a telephone call from someone else who was there. He was greatly excited. "I just wanted you to know what has happened," he said. "Larry got a call about a job as soon as he got back from the retreat. They have had a preliminary interview and they like him. It looks like the job is his, and we are all so thrilled that we wanted you to know about it, too!" In yielded and childlike trust, and in the bringing of our concerns to God in prayer, God does "open the windows of heaven" to give us this day our daily bread.

Give us this day our daily bread also means that as we are in the service of God, and that we are responsible also for making it come true for others. There are literally hundreds, if not thousands of organizations helping to feed the hungry of the world. Some are concerned with direct feeding, such as the projects known as "Meals for Millions" and CARE. Sometimes we can help by contributing to causes that send technical help to foreign countries, helping people to help themselves. There are local organizations to help the poor and underprivileged in every city and town. When possible, a little money here and a little there can do much to alleviate deprivation and want. All such organizations can remind those who think they are forgotten that someone cares. These organizations could not exist without our help, and I believe it is only as we do help that we can truly pray, "Give us this day our daily bread."

It is good, and it takes so little, to support an orphan overseas. For only a few dollars a month, a child will be able to eat or go to school. This money is not wasted; it enriches the whole world. If our hands and feet and minds are the only hands and feet and minds that God has on this earth, then we are the visible means that an invisible God uses to do His work on earth. Jesus is our example. He was the incarnate nature of God, our example of what God would do if God were in human form. Our commission is *to do likewise.*

Give us this day our daily bread means that God is involved in our entire economic life. The provident expression of His nature created the world (and they that dwell therein) in such a manner that the economic supply of our needs is built into the structure of His world. Just as He provides the physical necessities and satisfactions of all creatures—the bird and the fox and the ear of corn and the flower—so He also has provided for human economic needs. The physical and the material are as "religious" as any other facet of living. Abundant living is a right relationship with all life, and it is evidence of a free expectancy and a bold claiming of what is rightfully ours by the will of the Creator.

When we say, "Give us this day our daily bread," we should say it with the arms of expectancy stretched out to receive, and with our hearts bursting with gratitude, adoration, and love for the beneficence of God. In seeking first the Kingdom of God we cultivate and attune ourselves to the abundancies of heaven, and make friends with them. If we seek them, we shall surely find them.

Give us this day our daily bread means the discovery of God operating, guiding, and providing in our entire economic structure. He is always there, waiting to "burst out like a flood," "*by our hand,*" if we will but provide Him a channel of manifestation by our asking, expectancy, claiming, and serving.

7

Forgive Us Our Trespasses, as We ...

THESE words express Jesus' attitude toward the whole area of social relationships.

No man lives alone. Much as he might like to delude himself that he is all that matters to himself, it is simply not true. Even the cloistered monk needs the companionship of others like himself. He may withdraw from the normal round of social living, but it is only a matter of degree. The need for others is even more pronounced with those of us who remain in society. Periodic retreats from the press of modern living are necessary to keep inviolate our individual identity, but our individual identity soon loses all meaning when it is completely separated from others. When a man has gone too far along the road of withdrawal, he is in need of psychiatric help.

Just as the *Kingdom* of heaven connotes a *society*, our earthly life is a reflection of it in that we are social beings. Part of the training of our lives is to learn to live as social beings, related to each other, and necessary to each other—or else we shall be unprepared and unfitted for citizenship in the spiritual realm we call the Kingdom of Heaven.

Forgive us our debts as we forgive our debtors is an uncomfortable statement, and in many ways it is rather impossible if looked at from the human point of view. We say it with our lips, but our actions demonstrate that we do not take it too seriously. If we really believed that our relationship with God was dependent upon our relationship with other people, and if we truly thought that any possibility of heaven (the perfect fulfillment of life here and in the hereafter) would be determined by how we get along with other people, social relationships would not be in the state of tension that we find them.

However, there is another way of looking at this conception of the Lord's Prayer, and I think it is more true to the attitudes of Jesus. The starting point is not men, but God. *A right and harmonious relationship with God will result in a right relationship with people.*

Some years ago a young married woman came to a minister, another man, and myself. We were speakers at a conference and she had made an appointment with us. Her story was not unusual. Unfortunately marriage problems are not out of the ordinary. In this particular family they were pronounced to the extreme. In desperation she had come to the conference, hoping for something to give her a reason to go on living, and to make something of her life and the lives of her children. She evidently had little hope of anything being done about her husband and her marriage.

As she told us of years of unhappiness it became obvious that the young woman herself was in dire need of a right relationship with God. Patching up her marriage piece-meal, even if it had been possible, would have made it only endurable at best.

We began to talk to her about God and Jesus Christ. At first she resisted any effort to change the subject, but in kindness we persisted. We told her that her main problem was not with her husband, but within herself. If she could get herself straightened out, she would be more able to cope with her marriage.

Little by little she became more receptive, and finally she got down on her knees and recommitted her life into the hands of God. Deep peace settled in the room. The majestic silence of rest reigned supreme. A few tears of joy ran down her cheeks and the tortured and haunted look in her face gave way to something quite beautiful and childlike. Her appearance was actually transformed before our eyes. She stood up, and with joy written all over her face, said, "Oh, I must telephone my husband. I have to talk with him and ask him to forgive me for all the things I have done. He has really been so patient and kind over the years."

That is exactly what she did. I saw the couple some years later, and from all they said, and from what I could see, they had a normally happy home life. What had been accomplished in a few hours could not have been accomplished in many months by the usual method of psychological or marriage counseling.

The point of the story is that when the woman got into a right relationship with God, she automatically got into a right relationship with her husband. When we are unforgiving with other people, it is a symptom of our being separated from God. Forgiveness is coming into a condition of harmony with another. It does not mean that we approve of, or even agree with, the other person, but it does mean that we do not hate or resent him; nor do we wish him harm.

A judge in Oklahoma, some years ago, had to sentence a man to death for murder. He summarized the man's past life. The man had been discriminated against in a most atrocious manner from childhood. He had been mistreated at home, in school, and apparently by the law until he was bound by hate and went deeper into a life of crime that eventually led to murder and the sentence of death. The judge castigated society, and though it was necessary to pass the death sentence he was heartsick about it. That was an example of having to punish, and even cause death, but there was no hate involved in the feelings and attitudes of the judge. There was no wish to harm; there was a wish to help, but in that case it was not possible.

Forgive us our trespasses, as we forgive those who trespass against us carries with it the realization, in the mind of Jesus, that we must not permit our social relationships to destroy our relationship with God. It is all too easy to become so involved with people that we let them capture our interest and energies to the exclusion of everything else, including God.

A woman came home from a shopping center livid with anger one Saturday afternoon. She said that someone had "ignored" her. The one she was complaining about was a person she yearned to have as a friend. Because her mind was fixed so much on the actions of the one she wanted as a friend, any action that the other person made was interpreted as something personally related to her. When she was questioned about what happened at the shopping center, she said that she had called to the other woman and had been "ignored." Under more questioning it was shown that the shopping center was crowded by the influx of Saturday shoppers. We asked her if it was not possible that her friend did not see her, and that she did not hear her. After a little talking she agreed that this was not only possible but probable. Yet she had allowed the incident to ruin her afternoon when there was no need for it.

As long as we give people the place that only God ought to have in our lives, we are bound to get hurt. Indeed, it would be a tragedy if anyone were able to take the place of God in our lives. If the center of our lives were within ourselves instead of in other people, others would not be so important to us. When other people become a God-substitute, we have opened the gates of disappointment.

Unforgiveness adds burdens which eventually become so heavy that we are forced to our knees. I met a young man in his twenties who had lived a life of crime. Beatings and hunger were the common experiences of his childhood; love and understanding were apparently unknown to him. Under the circumstances it seems only natural that he was in almost constant trouble with the police. The patience of the police and the courts soon wore themselves out. He was in and out of correction houses, and then in and out of prison. He acquired the habit of hate, and anything to do with authority and respectability aroused resentment in him.

Someone paid his way to a religious summer conference. He was not remotely interested in religion, but it was a good chance to get a free vacation, and so he went. One evening toward the end of the week we went for a ride in the car. He wanted to talk. Association with kindly people had done something to him. For one week he had lived with kindness and happiness and cleanliness. Listening to talks and attending prayer groups had caused him to begin thinking along a different line.

We parked the car alongside a country road and he was soon spewing out all the resentment and venom of a lifetime. From his own point of view, he had plenty of reason to hate. His attitude was understandable, but that did not make it any more bearable. The misery of a young life was laid bare. It is doubtful that it had ever happened before, and perhaps in the telling of it he saw himself for the first time. At least he had never questioned his hate before. Now he was reaching out for help. Even though he could see no way out of it, his heart told him there was a different way.

"What can I do?"

"I think you know the answer," I said. "We have talked about forgiveness this past week. It was the only part of the Lord's Prayer that Jesus re-emphasized. He said that if we do not forgive others, God will not forgive us. He did not say that it might be a good idea if we forgive others. It was almost a 'Do it, or else!'"

"But," he said, "how is it possible to get over feeling the way I do?"

"It hasn't got anything to do with feelings. We are to walk by faith and not by our feelings. Walk by faith and the feelings will take care of themselves at the right time. The doing of something often has to take place before feelings change. The practice and the habit will produce their own feelings. Jesus said, 'not every one who says to me, "Lord, Lord," shall enter the kingdom of heaven, but he who does the will of my Father who is in heaven.'"

"How do I do it?"

"Well, let's start this way. First of all, be willing, by faith, to let go of all your resentment and unforgiveness. Make up your mind that you want to travel a different road in life."

"I want it, or I wouldn't be here with you."

"All right; as you are willing, in spite of your feelings, let's do it this way. I have some paper here and I want you to write down all the things you remember that you have to be forgiving about. Go back as far as you can remember and write down everything."

"It will take all night," he blurted out.

"If it takes all night, I have the time and so do you. You don't have to go into detail in the writing. Just a word or two will bring it all to mind, but do it as completely as you can."

He began writing. He would stop to think, and again he would scribble on the paper. After a long, long time he said,

"I think this is it. I can't think of anything more."

"Fine," I said. "Now just write down at the bottom something that says this paper also includes all the other unforgivenesses that you cannot remember right now."

When he had done this, I told him to read the list to me; it was not necessary to go into detail. I suppose it was a form of confession, both to God, who represented all that we mean by life (visible and invisible), and to myself, representing humanity. It took quite a while.

"You have carried these burdens along with you for a very long time," I told him. "Now the time has come to let them go. You are not going to spend any more energy thinking about them, hating, being resentful and emotionally disturbed over them. You are going to give them to God. We'll stand out in the roadway here, and you will perform an act of faith by touching a match to them; and as they burn and the smoke rises in the air it is going to be an act of worship. You are obeying Jesus Christ and God, and that is real worship. In a symbolic way the rising smoke will be like incense before the altar of God. All the hate and anger and resentment of a lifetime will be transformed into prayer."

He went out to the middle of the roadway, crumpled the papers, lit them with a match, and stood there silently as they were transformed to ashes and smoke. Soon there was nothing left but a few black ashes which he crumpled to dust in his hand and blew into the night air. He stood there in silence for some time and then he turned and raised his arms, as a bird lifts her wings, and in a voice choked with emotion he said, "I feel so light—*so light!* It's as if I didn't have any weight at all—as if I could really fly. I feel so good. I can't ever remember feeling this good—and God is so close!"

Forgiveness is letting go of burdens! No wonder the young man felt so light. Letting go of burdens is setting ourselves free.

We would be wrong to assume, because Jesus said that God would not forgive us unless we forgave others, that God is temperamental, insisting on His own way merely for the sake of getting His own way. Such a conception of God would be unworthy of the God revealed by the personality and body of Jesus Christ.

Suppose someone went to a track coach and said that he wanted to be a runner; and suppose this young person insisted upon carrying a heavy stone around with him. The first thing the coach would do would be to tell him to let go of the rock. Perhaps the imaginary conversation would be something like this:

"Fine. I can make you a runner, but first of all you've got to let go of that rock."

"I can't do it. I've carried it around with me for so long that I'm used to it. It is part of me."

"No, I'm sorry, you've got to let go of that rock if you want to be a runner."

"You're being temperamental! You just want to do it your way. I want to be a runner but I want to keep my rock."

"No, it can't be done that way. Either drop it or I won't teach you."

"There you go again. You keep saying, 'I won't.' You're temperamental!"

"I only say, 'I won't,' as another way of saying that I am not able to make a runner of you while you insist on keeping a heavy stone. To be a runner you have to get rid of every weight that is unnecessary. It isn't that I don't want to help you. You make it impossible for me to help you."

As God is Love, as love is the law of life, *we make it impossible* for that love and goodness to invade us when we are unforgiving. *We* have closed the doors of communication. God is not only forgiving; *God is forgiveness.* It is His nature. We have to permit that forgiveness, we have to be willing to have it. There may be many laws in life that we do not like, but if we want to reap the benefits of them we must cooperate with them. The forgiveness of our trespasses as we forgive the trespasses of others is a law of life, and like all laws it is neither changed nor compromised simply because we may not like it, or are unused to it.

Forgiveness must become *a way of living.* It may begin as a technique for saving oneself from hurt or for one's mental survival, but for full and free living it must become as natural as the air we breathe. A technique is like an artificial appendage that we utilize for our own benefit. We have to think about using it. It is not natural for us and, because of this, it is a source of drained energy and unnatural tension. When the time comes that we do not "have forgiveness" but actually "become forgiveness," then and only then are we in the land of social liberty and personal freedom.

Once when Jesus told the disciples that there was no end to forgiveness they said, "Increase our faith" (Luke 17:5). In other words, they considered it a practically impossible standard of achievement. Then Jesus told them the story about a man and his servant. The two had worked in the fields all day long. When they came home at night the master did not ask the servant to sit down while he served him. No, the servant quite naturally served his master, and he did not think he had done something worthy of commendation in doing it. It was his job; there was nothing out of the ordinary in it at all. So, said Jesus, when we have done all these things, we can say to ourselves, "We are unworthy servants . . ." (Luke 17:10, RSV).

This takes the matter of forgiveness entirely out of the area of emotionalism. Like a man in the armed services, we are under orders; it has nothing whatever to do with how we feel. Personal tiredness or impatience is beside the point. We have a job to do, and our personal feelings will only get mixed up in it if we permit them to do so.

In disciplined and almost military obedience we will discover a great secret: obedience to a universal law will produce its own feelings. Feelings are the *result* of something; they are not independent realities in themselves; they result from something else. One who strikes another man will find certain feelings as a result of that blow. There might be a momentary exhilaration, but you can be sure it will be followed by remorse in some form or other. For the one who indulges in brutal habits, brutalizing feelings and attitudes must always be the result. One is the natural result of the other. So the law is irrevocable. It is just as true in the matter of forgiveness. *Forgiveness carries with it its own resultant feelings.* To forgive is to come into a harmonious relationship with the nature of God the Creator, and to come into a harmonious relationship with the nature of the Creator is to come into that same kind of relationship with His creation. Intimacy, warmth, ease, peace, and joy are some of the natural results of it; in general, "the fruit of the Spirit . . ." (Galatians 5:22-23, RSV).

Forgive us our trespasses, as we forgive those who trespass against us implies that our primary consideration is our own forgiveness by God. Our own heart-hunger for God is the driving motivation. The compulsion to end the sense of separation we are aware of forces us to seek forgiveness and oneness. We are lonely and dissatisfied and we know that the cause of it is an inner loneliness for God. In the process we often tend to separate the visible from the invisible, society and the world of the senses from the spirit. According to the knowingness of Jesus, the here and the now—the present society in which we are physically involved—and the Godward urge must not be separated. Nevertheless, our basic, instinctive knowing is correct—God is the answer to our needs.

Forgive us our trespasses, as we forgive those who have trespassed against us makes a union of the world of the spirit with the world of social relationships. This reflects the entire attitude of Jesus in the first half of the Lord's Prayer where the emphasis is: ". . . in earth, as it is in heaven." They must merge; the inner and the outer must become one. So it is that Jesus once told the story about a man taking his gift to the altar. Evidently the man was religious; he was, perhaps sincerely, living up to the demands of his religion and church membership. He brought his gift to the altar, but that was not enough in the mind of Jesus. Jesus said, "So if you are offering your gift at the altar, and there remember that your brother has something against you, leave your gift . . . and go; first be reconciled to your brother, and then come and offer your gift" (Matthew 5:23-24, RSV). Religious ritual and practices, unless manifested in social relationships, are meaningless. At best they delude us into thinking we are right with God, and as such do us harm.

In another part of the New Testament the Apostle James tells us that love and the feeding of your brother go hand in hand; that to say, to love your brother and to let him go hungry is not love at all. So, too, to say or indulge in practices that indicate you are in a right relationship with God, and to be out of relationship with your brother—to be angry with him, to withhold yourself from him, to point your finger at him in derision, or to try to harm him—is meaningless and completely opposed to the nature of God as revealed by the words and actions and incarnation of Jesus of Nazareth. Such attitudes and practices would be utterly foreign to His nature.

Many times in the gospels Jesus was at sharp variance with the scribes and the Pharisees over this very point. Those men were religious to the extreme, deeply concerned over rites and traditions, and yet they had missed the point of their practices. All their rituals were supposed to indicate that a man was in union with the nature of God; they were supposed to be the means and techniques whereby men would maintain a close relationship with God. Sadly enough, the practices and rituals had become an end in themselves.

The prophets fought against the same spiritual malady. Many people are still doing battle with the same problem. Man has a propensity to substitute rituals and observances for the living of a life, a form for the spirit. It is much easier and makes us inwardly complacent. At the extreme, it is a drug that deadens us to the needs about us while at the same time it makes us appear to ourselves and others as a person in a right relationship with God. To some outsiders it gives religion a bad name and holds it up to ridicule. Others, assuming that this is a true expression of religion, dismiss it as superstitious and ineffective.

In Matthew 23:23 we read, "Woe unto you, scribes and Pharisees, hypocrites! for ye pay tithe of mint and anise and cummin, and have omitted the weightier matters of the law, judgment, mercy, and faith: these ought ye to have done, and not to leave the other undone."

Jesus was not quarreling with ritual and observances. In fact He said that they ought to be remembered and practiced. He was criticizing the scribes and Pharisees, and in a rather cutting manner, for neglecting what the ritual is supposed to symbolize and imply—justice, mercy, and faith. In the mind of Jesus the ritual and the spirit, the form and the attitude, were one and the same.

The matter of forgiveness was so important to Jesus that when life was at its worst for Him—when He was hanging on the cross, an object of pain, rejection, and brutality—He voiced forgiveness: "Father, forgive them; for they know not what they do" (Luke 23:34). Forgiveness was a *way of life* with Him. It permeated His entire spiritual and mental outlook. It colored His total attitude. He *was* forgiveness, and this forgiveness had to include the world as well as the Kingdom of God. Both had to be merged into a new creation. Such was His mind.

An old friend of mine once told a story about a man who was a farmer. One day he was plowing in a field with a mule, and the mule was not doing what the man wanted him to do; he would not walk in a straight line and he was plowing across the furrows as much as alongside them. In sheer exasperation the man ran up to the mule and punched him on the nose so hard that it drew blood. Immediately he was ashamed of himself and wished with all his heart that the incident had not taken place. Swept with guilt he got down on his knees in the field and asked God to forgive him, but he did not get any peace. He continued to pray, but the shame and guilt still held him. He could think of no more words to say and simply remained silently on his knees. Then it was as if a voice spoke into his mind and said, "Don't ask Me for forgiveness—ask the *mule*." With deep sincerity the farmer did so, and immediately the shame and guilt lifted.

It is not enough to ask God for forgiveness, basic and necessary as this is. We also have to do something, whenever possible, to make things right with those with whom we have been unforgiving. This does not mean that we are to seek out people and tell them what we have been doing to them, or thinking about them, or trying to do to them. (Sometimes this can be a backhanded way of telling people what we really think of them while hiding behind the cloak of religion.) We have no right to inflict pain on anyone else merely to make ourselves feel better, but there are many times when setting right what we have made wrong is well within our means. Certainly when others know what has been going on, we are in a position to ask forgiveness if we really mean it. And, remember, it is not necessary for those other people to say that they forgive us. They do not have to forgive us in order for us to obtain forgiveness; we are already forgiven when we ask for it. We have cleared the barriers that separate us from them, whether or not they have cleared the barriers that separate them from us.

The story of the Prodigal Son throws wonderful light on forgiveness. It is the story of everyone's life. The younger son wanted his inheritance in order to go out into the world and enjoy himself. In one sense the world is our inheritance, and our desire is to go out and take it for our own enjoyment. When the prodigal son's life had turned into disaster we come to the turning point of the story: "And when he came to himself . . ." (Luke 15:17).

Others may help us along the road of coming to ourselves, but the final realization has to come from within ourselves. It is eventually an "inside job" and not an "outside job."

Important as this inner realization is, there is more; there is thought. The prodigal son remembered his home and the safety and security of those who worked for his father, and he decided that he would be much better off as a servant of his father than where he was. Notice that in this story there is no hint of emotionalism, no weeping and no beating of the breast in agony and despair. Perhaps the son was even beyond that. There can come a time in life when things are so bad that we are incapable of worry. We are completely defeated, too defeated to worry or weep.

After surveying the situation, the young man said, "I will arise and go to my father, and will say unto him, Father, I have sinned against heaven, and before thee, And am no more worthy to be called thy son: make me as one of thy hired servants" (vv. 18-19). He knew what he ought to do, and he knew the way to do it. But even that is not enough. All of us know many things that we do not do, and the knowing and the "not doing" can make us even more miserable than when we were ignorant. The young man did not fall into that trap. "And he arose, and came to his father" (v. 20). His get-up-and-go "got up and went." He *did* it!

And now comes the important part of this story as regards the subject of forgiveness. "But when he was yet a great way off, his father saw him, and had compassion, and ran, and fell on his neck, and kissed him" (v. 20). *The father saw and loved him before the son knew anything about it.* In the son's mind, he was doing it all; but in reality he had merely placed himself in a position to receive what was *already there.* The lesson of the story is that God is always forgiving, because He is forgiveness.

"But," someone once said to me, "what about our asking for forgiveness? We are told to confess our sins and to ask forgiveness."

Perhaps it can be illustrated in this manner. When one of my sons was little, we were very close to each other. We showed our affection for each other naturally and easily. At night I often went up to bed with him. Stories were told, we shared the experiences of the day, we laughed, and we lay together on the bed at the close of the day and prayed together. Then he did something that was wrong. It did not really amount to anything, but he knew he should not have done it. I knew he had done it but I had not said anything about it. As the days went by, he withdrew from me little by little. He was much more quiet than usual. The natural lightness of his personality was darkened and dampened. I would notice him outdoors and every so often he would sadly look off into space. He was miserable, and the more miserable he became, the more I was conscious of him; and the more he hurt, the more I hurt. I wanted to go to him and tell him I knew all about it, but I also knew it would have to come from him. Of course, if it had gone too far I would have taken the initiative. The time came when his interior burden got to be too much for him and one day he threw himself in my arms and cried, "Daddy, forgive me," and told me all about it. Of course I said, "Yes, I forgive you."

Now the whole point here is that I had nothing to forgive him for—if by "forgiving" one means that I had been unforgiving. In a sense he had "sinned" against the laws of the household, and as Isaiah says, "Your sins have separated *you*. . . ." God has not withdrawn. God has not changed. The quality of His nature has not changed. It is *man* who has withdrawn.

It was also necessary for my little boy to ask for forgiveness. It had to be confirmed in *his mind*. He had to know, consciously. His asking was *his willingness* to accept what was *always there*. My answer was the spoken revelation of *my nature;* that too was *always there*. My answer was also *important;* it was the conscious confirmation *of his deep desires—forgiveness*.

The dialogue of the soul with God is exactly the same as it was with my son and me. The separation is bridged; love and acceptance are restored; ease of relationships is spontaneous; contentment and inner rest sweep clean the personality. One is at home.

The subject of forgiveness applies to events as well as people. Unforgiveness is the habit or the desire of shutting out someone or something. It is fighting the flow of life toward us as if life were our enemy.

A woman who is a fine artist told me of her experience with the telephone. It seemed that whenever she was busy working on a painting, the phone would ring and her work was constantly being interrupted. Soon she found herself actually hating the telephone and disliking the people who were using it to interrupt her work. She knew that was wrong, and determined to do something about it. She would welcome the telephone! Every time it would ring she said, "Thank you, Father." What she meant was that, as she was God's child, He would not permit anything to happen that would really hurt her. The robe of His nature was such, inside and outside of her, that only what was in harmony with His nature could get through to her—and that included the telephone. She said that it was not long before her life, which had become bitter and resentful, was once more open and she welcomed all of life.

Do something kind for someone you have been out of sorts with. A woman who had been active in church work found it almost impossible to get along with another woman. No matter what she said or tried to do, it seemed that the other woman blocked it, or at least robbed it of its joy. A fine woman found herself giving in to resentment, anger, and hurt.

"You know," she told me, "it sounds quite silly, but I went down to the florist and brought that woman a plant. I knew she loved flowers. I didn't include a card with it, but I think she knew, for our relationship began healing from that very moment."

Albert Cliffe used to say that if life was not good for you it could usually be traced to some case of unforgiveness. He would say that you should look at your relationships with other people, that somewhere you "had your foot on the hose." He meant that we were blocking the channels of God's constant flow to us, and his experience told him that it usually had something to do with unforgiveness.

Newton Dillaway once wrote a book called *Consent*. The idea of it was that we must not give in to resentment about life. "Consent" was the secret word that explained release to him. In other words, do not fight it; "consent" to life and everything that comes along by the faith that "God is in it all." It changed Dillaway's life, and it will change anyone's life when they catch the secret and practice it.

Jesus told us that no one came to Him except by the Father, and that He could, therefore, not deny them. We must assume something of the same sort about people who come into our lives, if Jesus is the perfect picture of the God-filled personality involved in social relationships. There is a reason for those who come into our lives. When we deny them we are attempting to play God. What we are attracts and it repulses. If we are in harmony with God, then we had better make up our minds to accept those who are attracted to us with a trust that rests in God. To shut ourselves off from life is to shut life off from ourselves, and therefore to separate ourselves from God.

Forgive us our trespasses, as we forgive those who trespass against us means that we need God's help, and it means that we are conscious of needing God's help. It also reminds us that life on earth, and especially our relationships with others, is heavenly business.

8

And Lead Us Not Into Temptation, but Deliver Us From Evil

PROBABLY no phrase in the Lord's Prayer has caused more confusion than this one. The problem comes from our identification of temptation with that which is evil, or an allurement to that which is base and sinful. Certainly when one uses the word in conversation it almost automatically elicits the connotation of sin.

We must differentiate here between sin and something that may lead to sin, but is not sinful in itself. In fact, we have to recognize that anything may lead to sin. Many times we blame the instrument of testing rather than ourselves. There is something of Adam and Eve in all of us—"The woman . . . gave me of the tree, and I did eat," or "The serpent beguiled me, and I did eat" (Genesis 3:12, 13). It is much easier on our consciences that way.

The clue to a reasonable understanding is in our interpretation of "temptation." A perfectly good definition is that it is "testing." This interpretation corresponds with what we know about all of life. Testing is a necessity of living. We test wood, steel, and stone in order to find out what they are capable of supporting. We test our ability to read, to run, and to think, but no one therefore calls them evil. We find out something about ourselves, even if that something is not always complimentary. Everything in life is tested in some manner. According to what we know of the nature of God the Creator, we must consider that testing, or temptation, is good. It is there to help us, to instruct us, and to make us stronger.

Temptation as *testing* is common throughout the Bible. Abraham was tempted to offer his son in sacrifice, and from the tempting he grew in spirit and understanding. He was the stronger for it.

Jacob and his mother yielded to the temptation to acquire the inheritance that was not legally his. At a later time he found out that he could no longer depend upon his wits and cunning, and threw himself into the hands of God.

Moses was tempted by the enormity of his task of leading the children of Israel out of Egypt, and he wanted to die. Death as a way out of difficulties was his temptation, or testing, and he learned from it that death is not the way out. It meant a renewed relationship with his God and a reiteration of the Source of his strength.

Elijah also prayed that he might die, and that was his testing. He was tested or tempted to believe that he was the only one left in his own country who was faithful to God. From the testing he came out chastened but stronger.

There are temptings or testings of all sorts in the Bible, and this is but a reflection of what the program of living entails. Testing is part of life. It is a good part of life and it is a necessary part of life, not to destroy us, but to make us wiser, stronger, and more responsible.

It is only in this connection that we can believe the statement of the gospels that Jesus was "led of the spirit" into the wilderness to be *tempted* by Satan (Matthew 4:1). If there was anything intrinsically evil in the act of tempting, one cannot imagine it originating with God. Temptation is likely the only way that we shall truly know ourselves as we really are. Virtue is of little value if we are sheltered from the stresses and strains of life, encased in some sort of environmental test tube and shielded from doubts and uncertainties. We would never know ourselves.

Every man has his breaking point. Sometimes it is mental, and sometimes it is spiritual, and sometimes it is physical. The area of one's life that is likely to break before another is not the same with all people. There is a story of a Roman Catholic priest who was arrested by the Chinese Reds and put into solitary confinement. Others had broken under such extreme isolation. However, the priest seemed to thrive upon it. Eventually he was let out.

Friends asked him how he was able to stand it. He smiled and said, "I have yearned for more solitude for years. I came to China as a missionary. As the work succeeded, more and more administrative duties were forced upon me. You have no idea how much I have wanted solitude over these years. The little I have been able to snatch for myself has been much too meager. Before I came to China I had time for such a lot of it. So, you see, if the Reds had tried to think of something I would really appreciate, they could not have done a better job than this."

Lead us not into temptation, but deliver us from evil is but another way of saying, "*Dear God, deliver us from ourselves.*" It is all well and good to be in a proper relationship with our economic and social life, but ultimately a man has to live with himself. Life is arranged in such a way that no man is sufficient unto himself. If he were, he would need neither God nor his fellow man. The greatest battles we will ever face will be with ourselves; the greatest victories we will ever win will be over ourselves. The most disappointing defeats we will ever taste will be those in which we find we have defeated ourselves.

It may also be said that the answer to the prayer about daily bread and the one about forgiveness is only possible if this one is answered or adequately resolved. Until a man has a balanced view of himself, it can hardly be expected that he will have a balanced view of his economic and social relationships.

A young married woman found life well-nigh intolerable for her. She said that her husband was kind to her, and loved her. As far as she knew, those she worked for treated her as she ought to be treated. Yet her life was not worth living. She was miserable. Her periods of despondence were coming more frequently and lasting longer, and she feared for her sanity. In spite of the patience and love of her husband, they did not have a happy home life. "I am ruining it for him and for myself too," she sobbed.

The trouble was that she had a desperately severe case of inferiority feelings. Her older sister had been petite and vivacious, and everyone was attracted to her and made much over her. By contrast, she had been tall and gawky. She wanted to be like her sister. There was nothing about herself that she liked; she could not accept herself. She had tried blaming it on "life," but that did not help matters. All she had been able to do was to dream up excuses for the misery she experienced day by day.

The temptation in her life was to wish to be someone else. The test was to find some way of accepting herself. To run away from weakness (in any form) does not solve it, nor does it transform the weakness into a strength. She found her way out eventually by realizing that, like her sister, she too was made in the image and likeness of God, and that with God's help she could and would manifest the beauty placed there by the Creator Himself. As this truth became a living reality, her economic and social relationships improved by themselves. Basic to these improvements was the relationship that she had found with herself.

Lead us not into temptation, but deliver us from evil means that a man has come to the realization that there are qualities and proclivities within himself that he dare not trust himself to handle. He has come to know himself. A man told me that he simply could not go near any place where gambling was going on. He had had enough experience with himself to know that he did not have the stamina of character to take gambling in a moderate sense. It always meant going "all the way." At one time in his life he had had to go to jail because he bet money that he did not have, and his family had to suffer for it. It was a fever with him. There was no way he could explain it to himself, let alone anyone else.

With another person it might be alcoholic beverages. Alcoholics Anonymous says that one of the most important steps to sobriety is when a man calls upon a Higher Power. Here again is where a man says, in reality, "Dear God, save me from myself." It is a wise man's prayer. Socrates said, "Know thyself." When a man does, he knows that he is in need of help.

The testings of life come in varied and many forms, but they all lead to the same conclusion. We need help to control ourselves, to make the right decisions and not lower our standards of rightness. We need it as much when we are well-to-do as when we are poor-to-do. A family in a destitute country has as much strain obtaining a nickle to feed a child as does the family in this country who wonder where they are going to get the money to send a child to college. The person who is being put out of his room for want of ten dollars suffers as much as the man who cannot meet a large mortgage payment on a palatial home. And, in all of these, the temptation is there to achieve their goals by less than admirable methods.

The temptations of Jesus are universal to all mankind. As Jesus was "in all points tempted like as we . . ." (Hebrews 4:15), it is only natural that He should have had to face Himself, too. It makes little sense to believe that He was not *really* tempted and tested. It could not have been a mere philosophical or academic discussion; that is not real temptation. The temptations must have had an intense attraction for Him. How long they lasted, we have no idea. All we know is that they came to Him when He was weakened after fasting for forty days and nights; the Scripture says, ". . . and afterward he was hungry" (Matthew 4:2, RSV). Temptations always come at the point where we are susceptible and at the time when we are most prone to yield. Surely this fits in with the first temptation of food; there is little temptation to food if one's belly is full. "If thou be the Son of God, command that these stones be made bread" (v. 3).

It would be folly to think that food for the moment was the crux of the testing. Bread is but a symbol of our entire economic existence. It involves houses to live in, clothing to wear, and status in the community.

The successful businessman is the envy of most people. He lives in a large home, and he drives a good car. He belongs to the best clubs. He wears fine clothes. His children go to good schools. He usually sits on the board of his church. He takes his family on vacations that are not possible for the average person. He is well considered and looked up to when any serious problem of the community is reviewed. His success in business is the touchstone to all he has, and everyone wants to be like him.

In the first temptation of Jesus, the adversary is very cunning. He introduces the testing with the word "If. . . ." The first thing to do to get a person to yield to anything is to create a doubt: "*If* you are the Son of God . . ."—*If you are, do something* about it! Command that the stones be made into bread. *If you are so spiritual, why are you hungry?* If you are a child of God, *use Him* to satisfy your wants, regardless of what they are or how you came to be in your present condition. One does not necessarily follow the other, by any means.

Jesus was in this place, and in this condition, by His own free choice. He fasted to sharpen His thinking, clear His mind, and sensitize His spirit for great decisions. The ancient Hebrews also fasted in times of danger and crises; they fasted and they prayed. Apparently, as the physical forces of the body become weaker and more tenuous, clarity of thought and spirit are enhanced. We became more sensitive to awarenesses which are always there, but which are dulled by the forces of personality being used for the absorption of food.

Sundar Singh once began to doubt the reality of the spiritual world. Perhaps it was merely an illusion. He determined to find out. He went into the woods and fasted for forty days and forty nights. Some travelers found him in a state of semi-consciousness at the end of that time, or he might have died. However, he said it was worth it because as the fires of physical life burned lower and lower the spiritual realities became clearer and clearer. He never doubted the reality of the spiritual Kingdom of God again.

In the first temptation of Jesus we see the possibility of using spiritual laws or principles for ends for which they were not intended. Here was the temptation—not that stones could not be made into bread, but that it was a perversion of the heavenly (or life's) laws of supply and demand. Hunger could be satisfied in that manner, but there was no reason why Jesus could not have left the wilderness and gotten His daily bread in the normal and natural manner, like everybody else.

People are still tempted to do the same thing. One man told me that he had the ability to sit in his room and focus his attention upon people with the intention that they would send him money. By the use of his imagination and will, he would actually visualize someone coming to his room and giving him money "for his work." It would be foolish to assume that everyone he concentrated upon in such a manner fell victim to his misuse of imaginative demand; but apparently enough did so that he was able to live. There is a temptation to use such abilities, honed to a fine-edge skill, for personal benefit. Most such people begin their quest for life's meaning with the highest ideals and purest motives. They actually have spent time in prayer and meditation until they discover the power and possibilities that are there. Then comes the temptation to use such expert powers for their own benefit. They have been sidetracked. They have settled for something lower than their original goal. They have begun to play god, attempting to use others as they see fit. The time inevitably comes when it turns out disastrously.

Jesus realized the temptation in the wilderness. How long it took Him to overcome it, we do not know. To be a real attraction and a true temptation, it had to be a struggle. Maybe there was the rationalization that feeding the hungry was a worthy purpose. One who really had such power would, or could, undoubtedly do a lot of good. The power or the money could be used for good. But He knew a better way. Put a man in a right relationship with God, and the life of God in the laws of nature, and creation is built in such a manner that food and shelter and clothing will automatically flow toward him.

Jesus had the answer: "Man shall not live by bread alone, but by every word that proceeds from the mouth of God" (Matthew 4:4, RSV). The answer seems to be that there is nothing wrong in the necessity of our economic life, but it must not be subordinated to bread *alone*. No matter how successful a man might be—or how unsuccessful—it is not enough. This too must be subordinated to a life. The temptation to stand alone, buttressed by economic security, is common to all men. Jesus met it, knew its attraction, rejected it, and overcame it with the answer that must be the answer of everyman: *"but by every word that proceedeth out of the mouth of God."* The reality of God, His indwelling Spirit, His communion and will, must reign supreme here as in every other area of living.

The second temptation of Jesus is also common to all men: "Then the devil took him to the holy city, and set him on the pinnacle of the temple, and said to him, 'If you are the Son of God, throw yourself down; for it is written, "He will give his angels charge of you," and "On their hands they will bear you up, lest you strike your foot against a stone" ' " (vv. 5-6, RSV).

Popularity and recognition make up the second temptation. We want to be wanted, to be liked, and to be loved. There is no quicker way to gather a crowd of adulating people than to do something that seems miraculous. It is the unusual person who has not been utterly thrilled by the crowds that press upon popular personages, be it a movie star, a great evangelist, a returning war hero, or a sports great. We all want people to take notice of us. Basically, I suppose, it is the need to be loved and to be made aware of that love.

An outstanding speaker once told me that one of the greatest temptations he had was to sway people merely for the sake of swaying them. He enjoyed it; it came easy to him. He had the knack of telling stories, either in public or private, that made people envy him.

"You know," he told me, "I have to be very careful of this talent. I use it too often merely to have people tell me how good I am. I have come to understand that verse of Scripture that says, 'Keep thy tongue from evil and thy lips from speaking guile.' I think I have little trouble with the evil part of that verse, but I do have to be on constant guard about speaking guile. I find that when I do it I know I am wrong, and I find that I lose that close walk with God that I want."

The desire to be liked and loved is common to us all. There is nothing wrong with it. We are created that way, made in the image and likeness of God. In some mysterious manner, apparently, God Himself needs or demands to be loved. It is stamped into all creation which was made by Him. According to Scripture, God is Love.

Once again the temptation is to pervert this inborn need and talent simply for its own sake, or to use it for our own ends. A lovely lady told me that her chief temptation along this line was to use her beauty and personality to get her own way. She was interested in children and had opened a school for the handicapped. That was good; there was nothing wrong with the projects she was vitally interested in. She had helped many, many good causes. By experience she found that she had the ability to be greatly liked and admired by many people. She used it for good, but she said the temptation often came to use it for something not as admirable. Her beauty and personality and brains could do untold good as long as she subordinated it to God. She was not always sure that she would be true to what she knew was right.

We have all known women and men who refuse to get old. They continue to dress as they did in their youth. They force manners and gestures upon themselves that are appropriate to a much younger age. They attend affairs that are for young people, and avoid any affairs for people their own age as they would the plague. It works for a while, but age and life have a way of catching up with everyone. Then they find out that they have to develop a beauty that is entirely their own, something that radiates from the inside. Once more, there is nothing wrong with the desire to be loved and admired. The trouble comes and the evil comes when such a desirable want becomes a person's God. "Thou shalt have no other gods before me" (Exodus 20:3) is one of the rules of life. It was not spoken only of idols. Whatever we bow down to and serve is our God.

When a person has a natural or achieved popularity and uses it for the good of his fellow man, he will always find happiness and inner peace. It is not enough to be loved and liked; the liking and the loving must have a purpose beyond themselves. It is well and good to learn the art of being loved and liked, but to have it and not to have a purposeful meaning in life leads to but another form of intemperance. Too often we think of drunkenness in relation to whiskey, but there is also a sort of drunkenness of popularity and love. To be unable to handle it, to be willing to do anything for it, makes a man little different from the alcoholic. The wrongness is not in the demand of our natures to be liked and loved; it is in our propensity to use it as a technique for self-satisfaction.

The answer to all these urges is the answer of Jesus: "*Thou shalt not tempt the Lord thy God*" (Matthew 4:7). Perhaps a better word here is not to "bait" or "test" God (the Spirit of Life). With free will built into life as it is, we have the permission of life, created by God, to test how far we can go.

Longing to be popular and accepted by the "gang" in high school, one young girl soon found that she was pregnant. Another girl in the same school organized a group that met once a week to hear an inspirational speaker and to pray. It is said that we should never criticise another until we have walked in his shoes for a month. Who is to tell the intensity of the hunger of the former young girl as compared to the latter? No matter, the fact still remains that there are limits, and to compromise our highest can only be carried so far without unfortunate results. Do not tempt God: do not use the laws and energies of life for purposes for which they were not intended.

Acceptance, love, or acclaim—we need to save ourselves from

these, too. The tempting must come to every man. We need the help of God to prevent ourselves from giving in to ourselves. The attraction is more intense for some than for others, but we are all subject to it.

Lead us not into temptation, but deliver us from evil. How much this statement encompasses! It forces each individual to come to terms with himself, to realize that he is his own most important problem. It means that finally each person must come to know that he, by himself, is dependent upon God, that he is unable to control and trust himself alone.

The third temptation of Jesus is also common to the lot of men and women on this earth: "Again, the devil took him to a very high mountain, and showed him all the kingdoms of the world and the glory of them; and he said to him, 'All these I will give you, if you will fall down and worship me.' Then Jesus said to him, 'Begone, Satan! for it is written, "You shall worship the Lord your God and him only shall you serve"'" (vv. 8-10, RSV).

Power! Who dares to say that he has not wished for it, not once, but many times. Power seems to be the ultimate in security. If we had enough power we would lose our fears, and our fears are what trouble us most. Fear of nonacceptance by others, fear of ourselves and our inferiorities, fear of others who might be able to lord it over us—all these we are sure could be overcome if we but had power, *real power.*

I have known men who have achieved immense success. One would imagine that they would then enjoy life by traveling, by improving themselves as they always said they would, and by helping others. Many times this is not true. The security of money and the joy of it are not what drives them on. It is power. They still continue to work as if they did not have it. They almost demand the challenge of forcing something to work—be it a new business enterprise or a new wife. They enjoy power for its own sake.

One man knelt down and cried because he would not be able to take his millions with him when he died. It was not comical; it was heart-rending. He had worked his way up over practically insurmountable handicaps and now ruled a vast industrial empire. He was the friend and confidante of senators, congressmen, clergymen; he was accepted in the best social circles. He had enough power to make people bend to his will, if necessary. There was one fact he could not reconcile himself to and that was that he would leave the world as naked as the day he entered it. With all the power he possessed and enjoyed he found it difficult to bow his knee to the God of the universe. He found out that there was still something a man had to bow his knee to. It was God, and eventually he did it.

How many times we have said, "If I were president!" We would make the world act as we believe it ought to act. We would force recalcitrant peoples and nations to conform to our image of what is right. We would then force the mayor, the minister, the doctor, the mechanic, the interior decorator, the driver of that other automobile—all of them—to toe the mark. Indeed we would—and is it not the wisdom of the universe that we do not have that power?

Of course, we could also do much good if we had that kind of power and used it rightly. We could impose our will that food be distributed so that the hungry all over the world could eat, and we could also make education necessary and available all over the world. We could force the nations of the world to live in cooperation with each other. There is so much we could do; but the rest of mankind would be living in virtual terror for fear that someone at some time would fall under the disfavor of the one who held that power—I or you.

Someone has said that power corrupts and absolute power corrupts absolutely. It is true. No one in the history of the world has been able to handle great power with the wisdom that he thought he could. A benevolent dictator is still a dictator; freedom for everyone else is lost.

Jesus once said that if we had faith as a grain of mustard seed we could tell a mountain to move and it would do so. No one has seen such faith, nor the power of it. However, how many people could be trusted with that sort of power? How comfortable and how secure would anyone feel if there were someone, like us, who actually had the power to move mountains? What about the mornings when he got up out of the wrong side of the bed? What about the moments when he lost his temper? What about the times, which come to everyone, when he wanted to show off? Is there really anyone you would trust with that sort of power, even yourself? I think not. Yet, when we see the seemingly impossible things that people do with the little faith they have, who is to say that the moving of mountains is not possible? But certainly not, by the wisdom and goodness of God, until we are ready to handle such power.

The Bible is full of stories of kings who were unable to handle the intoxication of power. The stories are so similar that there is little chance of not knowing the story of any one of the kings; they are all so similar. They became unfaithful to their highest visions. Saul became a great king, from rather meager circumstances, only to fall victim to what lay at the fingertips of any great king. David was not immune, great as he was, but David had the childlikeness and the honesty to say, "I have sinned. . . ." The story of all the kings is that they fell down and worshiped other gods. We do the same today. When we feel that we have achieved something, it is not long before we feel little necessity for God and a vision that is greater than ourselves. Sometimes we become our own god, and the satisfaction of our wants is the altar on which we sacrifice ourselves.

In recent history there is no clearer example of the urge to power than Adolf Hitler. From a beaten, neurotic, and laughable creature he came frightfully close to ruling the world. He dreamed it, he lived it, he imagined it, he worked day and night for it, he was ridiculed for it not only by his own people but by the world; and yet the "drive to power" came, nearly carrying the world with it. It ended in a Berlin bunker in flames and death. Surely this is an example of the drive for power gone berserk.

Jesus had to meet this test at the beginning of His mission, and He had to meet it again in later years. Once the people wanted to make Him a king, and He refused. His own disciples tempted Him with their requests to be one on His right-hand side and the other on His left when He came into His Kingdom. How many others had the same idea about His ministry, but did not actually say it to Him, is anyone's guess. Surely those two disciples were not the exception. The very fact that the incident made its way into the gospels is indicative that it was important to the writer. An isolated incident that had nothing to do with the rest of Jesus' ministry, one that was unrelated to the hopes of others, would be unlikely to make its way into the pages of the gospels. Jesus not only had to face up to this kind of possibility during the period of the temptations, but He had to face up to the normal attraction of power throughout His entire ministry.

The answer must always be the same if we are going to be able to live with ourselves in safety. Knowing ourselves as we really are means that we know we are prone to seek after power and that at the same time we are hardly able to be trusted with it. Power of sorts comes into the hands of everyone, no matter how small the territory it rules. How we handle it is all-important. God did not intend that a man should live on earth as a weakling; He intended that man should have dominion, and dominion means power. However, the dominion envisioned by God is a dominion by man who is at the same time in harmony and loving relationship with his Creator and all creation. The more any man knows of himself, the more he is aware that he needs help to protect himself from the God-implanted drives and needs that can be misused so easily.

Jesus' answers to the temptations come to the same conclusion, with slightly different emphases. A close, loving, trusting, and worshiping relationship with God is the answer to the cry of ". . . deliver us from evil" (Matthew 6:13).

One whose mind is filled with the consciousness of God will find little or no time for dwelling on the subject of evil and being trapped by it. The old hymn says, "Take time to be holy . . . Talk oft with thy Lord." It takes time to be holy, or to be whole and in a right relationship with God, just as it takes time to be anything. It also takes time to be unholy. Time is one thing we all have. The only choice we have in the matter is what we are going to do with it.

Dr. Frank Laubach carries a set of pictures of Jesus with him on his travels. Whenever he checks into a hotel he takes these pictures out and places them around his room. He sees them the first thing when he awakens in the morning; and he sees them the last thing before he goes to sleep at night. With all the associations and meanings that Jesus has for Frank Laubach, he has little time for low thoughts in such company!

The story is told in many different forms about the college boy who placed a picture of Jesus on the wall of his room. His mother had sent it to him, and out of love for her he put it up. It was not too long before his pin-up pictures disappeared—there are some things that do not go together! There are some thoughts and actions that do not fit with the company of Jesus.

Some people carry a picture of Jesus on their key chain, and they say it makes them better drivers. One man told me that he found it all but impossible to swear at other drivers with the picture of Jesus right there, *"looking at him!"*

Another man keeps a small picture of Jesus in his wallet. He finds it difficult and embarrassing to spend his money on certain items when that picture is a continual reminder that under God he is a steward of his money.

Many people find it helpful to carry with them something that reminds them of a higher reality and purpose in living. It does not have to be anything explicitly religious. A young man carries a small stone in his pocket; it was given to him by an old man who loved him and saw possibilities in him that he did not see in himself. At times he was tempted to do something that was far from his highest, but when he thought of his friend he would not do it. So one day he asked the old man for something, for anything, that he carried with him. It would help him to remember his old friend. The man took a small stone out of his pocket and gave it to him. The young man said to me, "You know, when I feel that stone in my pocket, I don't feel quite as alone, and I always try to be a better man."

So, one of the finest ways to be delivered from evil, or from the evil one, is to surround yourself with items or mementoes that remind you of God and the higher truths of life. You will not be so likely to live by bread alone, tempt God, or worship some idol, and therefore get into trouble.

Another good way to fill your mind and thoughts with the things and purposes of God is to memorize a Bible verse each day. There are all kinds of Bible promise-boxes. Place such a box on your kitchen table and pick out a promise each day. Either put it in your pocket or leave it on the table for the rest of the family to read. This simple act will give a brighter tone to the whole day.

A minister once told me, "I have found out that if I feed on the Word, the time comes when the Word feeds me." He meant that when he had filled his mind with Scripture, situations or times of need drew from his mind the words of comfort or courage that he needed. This reminds one of the story told about the missionary, David Livingstone. Once he was a captive in a tribal hut in Africa and it looked as if he would be killed the next morning. He began to give in to fear, when suddenly there flashed into his memory, "... lo, I am with you alway ..." (Matthew 28:20). Fear vanished and he gained control of himself almost immediately.

A good way to keep yourself God-centered is to associate with other people who are like-minded. A businessman told me that he found it invaluable to attend an early-morning prayer meeting and Bible study group every Monday. The subjects studied, and the practice of prayer itself, did a lot of good, but there was more. Many of the businessmen in the groups he had met before, but always in a business way. "The business world isn't quite as cutthroat to me any more, realizing that these businessmen are interested in the same things I am interested in," he told me.

The company of good spiritual literature is invaluable. Surely there is enough variety in religious books to satisfy anyone, regardless of their specific interest—from biography to prayer. Books are about the only way we have of sharing the thoughts of spiritual giants of the past and the present. Without a book, how would we ever know that Saint Augustine said, "Thou hast made us for thyself, and our souls are restless until they find their rest in thee." There are mental and spiritual treasures in books, and there is food for the soul. Fill your mind with the good thoughts of good books.

This section would be incomplete without a word about worship. The Scripture tells us not to forget "the assembling of ourselves together ..." (Hebrews 10:25). Public worship, as well as private worship, is of great benefit. Many people complain that they get so little out of public worship, but it is a necessity for full worship, nevertheless. It is too easy to withdraw into some kind of small religious club with yourself and perhaps a few other friends. Good as it is, it is not enough. The church, and the church in history, has meant too much to mankind for anyone to feel that either he is beyond it, or that it is not necessary.

A good friend of mine who was most critical of the organized church returned from a trip around the world and was simply enthusiastic about the church, what it has meant to the world, and what it is doing today. The organized church has started schools all over the earth, opened hospitals and medical centers, organized improved agricultural methods wherever it has gone, and laid the foundation for enlightened government. Through dark ages and light ages it has presented a witness to the world that no other institution can match. We strengthen ourselves, and all society, when we devote part of our worship of God to attendance in church.

Perhaps we can sum it up with some verses of Scripture: ". . . resist not evil. . . . but overcome evil with good" (Matthew 5:39; Romans 12:21). It has been said by others, many others, that ultimately God is good, and that ultimate good is God. Do not spend your time, your conscious thought, on evil, because whatever you give your time and thought to is bound to capture you. Give your all, time and thought, to a close walk with God, and deliverance from evil will take care of itself.

9

For Thine Is the Kingdom, and the Power, and the Glory, Forever. Amen.

MOST authorities agree that this last statement was not part of the original prayer, but that it was added by the early church and probably reflects the prayer of David in I Chronicles 29:11: "Thine, O lord, is the greatness, and the power, and the glory, and the victory, and the majesty: for all that is in the heaven and in the earth is thine; thine is the kingdom, O Lord, and thou art exalted as head above all."

This is a re-affirmation of the opening half of the Lord's Prayer. It brings us back to the Source after we have dwelled upon the problems each of us has to cope with here on earth. It reminds us once more that all things do come from God, that they are His, and that the problems of earthly living take their solution in Him.

An old song says, "Follow, follow, follow the gleam. . . ." It is necessary and wise to do so, for when the vision perishes we become wedded to the problems of earth rather than the overcomings of heaven.

A young man went to a speaker at a conference and, in detail, related all the things that were wrong with him. The conference leader suggested, "Why don't you meditate upon the overcoming power of God? You have permitted yourself to dwell upon your problems until you are the problem."

A puzzled look came over the young man's face as he said, "I don't know anything about meditation, and I don't know how to go about it." The leader replied, "You have been meditating on your problems for the past half-hour. It is simply thinking about something. When we talk about meditation we mean thinking about God instead of thinking of the affairs that have caused us so much worry and distress."

A man who owns an airport once told me that when the pressures of life got too great and he found himself reduced to fear, there was always something that greatly helped. He took one of the planes and spent an hour flying. The higher he flew, the smaller his problems became. In the stillness and aloneness and at the great height he felt close to God, and thought, "How small my problems must seem to my Heavenly Father. Truly all things are possible with Him, and nothing shall be impossible."

When one saturates his mind in the majestic glory and purposes of God, and when the things of earth are considered from this perspective, impossibilities are no longer impossibilities. He can face the problems of life with a courageous spirit and a serene mind, free of concern and fear.

The first half of the Lord's Prayer must never be separated from the last half because it is a *total attitude*, incapable of separation. There really is no first part and second part. Heaven and earth are one in the mind of the pray-er. The nature, Kingdom, and will of God is a present-tense reality that naturally conditions every facet of living in the here and the now. The two seemingly natural divisions of the prayer cannot be separated— first God and then life; they must be merged and lost in each other. Spirituality cannot be separated from materiality, and materiality cannot be separated from spirituality. The "new creation" of oneness begins within our own minds before it can be reflected in our outlook. This "at one-ment" becomes atonement because it results in oneness with God. The Lord's Prayer is the unconditional attitude of this oneness if it is lived and truly understood.

"For thine is the kingdom, the power, and the glory, forever. Amen," is but saying that the nature and the expression of God in creation is the supreme realization. It is a reminding of ourselves, and a rejoicing in ourselves, of the truth that is always here—imbedded in every atom, discovered in every fact of science, revealed in every great work of art, and displayed in every simple act of trust. It is the life in which we live and move and have our being.

For *Thine* is—

The Kingdom: A place, a condition, a manifestation, an unseen reality, a here and a now, a heretofore and a hereafter, a creative expression of the Creator, and the outpicturing of His nature.

And the Power: To sustain life, to create it, to drive it toward ends and goals, to remake it, to infill it, to give strength and meaning to it.

And the Glory: The magnificence of God that is reflected in nature, the universe, in every man and woman and child; the beauty, the balance, the temperance, the perfect timing, the infinite totality of perfection that is too much for comprehension.

Forever: The same yesterday, today, and forever; dependable and predictable, eternal, sure, unending.

Amen: It is so, it is truth, it is reality, it is realization, it is fact.